MW0117802Z

Pursuing Peace is like the sun breaking through on a cloudy day. These devotionals are heartfelt and full of wisdom. Each passage contains a beautiful deposit of inspiration and truth. They offer comforting reminders and teaching that brings new revelation, and words that prepare a place of peace for whatever the day may bring.

—Laura Woodley Osman
Worship Leader, Recording Artist, Author
www.spiritsoulbody.com

Ruth Teakle lives what she speaks and writes what she lives. I've known this faith-filled woman of wisdom, work, and wit for over twenty-five years. Jump in and enjoy her practical truths in *Pursuing Peace*, written in vivid, direct language for your encouragement and growth. As you do, the Holy Spirit will enable you to share that pursuit of peace with others.

—Rev. Melissa Bone
Author of *The Family Blessing Guidebook* and *Luke's Ladies*
Doula Practitioner, Blessing Births
blessingbirths.synthasite.com

You will love Ruth's conversational stories, which are personal and scriptural, especially during this time of COVID 19. Having walked through the many challenges of negative emotions associated with this past year, I literally felt the peace Ruth wrote of in each devotion. *Pursuing Peace* will be one of God's gifts to you through this season and beyond—a navigational guide through rough waters.

—Bev Hadland
Ordained Minister, Outreach Ambassador to the
First Peoples—Crossroads/100 Huntley Street
Author of the Best-Seller *Hang on to Your Hormones*
www.crossroads.ca/fpv/

Ruth demonstrates with great spiritual sensitivity how we can face our daily struggles and common hurts while knowing who we are in Christ. *Pursuing Peace* reminds us so beautifully of simple truths, such as how to: forgive and let it go, pursue peace, renew our mind, win with love, and trust in God's Word. These pages can be read over and over again—a wealth of testimony to be applied and treasured.

—Wendy Hagar
Founder and Director of Sew on Fire Ministries
2012 Burlington Citizen of the Year
Contributing Writer to *Faith, Life and Leadership Vol. 2*
www.sewonfire.com

Pursuing Peace

Pursuing Peace

A 30 Day Devotional Journey

Ruth Teakle
& a Company of Friends

PURSUING PEACE
Copyright © 2021 by Ruth Teakle

Unless otherwise indicated, scripture quotations are taken from the Holy Bible, NEW INTERNATIONAL VERSION®, NIV® Copyright © 1973, 1978, 1984, 2011 by Biblica, Inc.® Used by permission. All rights reserved worldwide. Scripture quotations marked (AMP) are taken from the Amplified® Bible, Copyright © 1954, 1958, 1962, 1964, 1965, 1987 by The Lockman Foundation. Used by permission. Scripture quotations marked (MSG) are taken from The Message. Copyright © by Eugene H. Peterson 1993, 1994, 1995, 1996, 2000, 2001, 2002. Used by permission of NavPress Publishing Group. Scripture quotations marked (ESV) are taken from The Holy Bible, English Standard Version® (ESV®), copyright © 2001 by Crossway, a publishing ministry of Good News Publishers. Used by permission. All rights reserved. Scripture quotations marked (NKJV) are taken from the New King James Version®. Copyright © 1982 by Thomas Nelson, Inc. Used by permission. All rights reserved. Scripture quotations marked (NLT) are taken from the Holy Bible, New Living Translation, copyright ©1996, 2004, 2007 by Tyndale House Foundation. Used by permission of Tyndale House Publishers, Inc., Carol Stream, Illinois 60188. All rights reserved. Scripture quotations marked (TPT) are taken from The Passion Translation®. Copyright © 2017, 2018 by Passion & Fire Ministries, Inc. Used by permission. All rights reserved. ThePassionTranslation.com. Scripture quotations marked (NASB) are taken from the New American Standard Bible®, Copyright © 1960, 1962, 1963, 1968, 1971, 1972, 1973, 1975, 1977, 1995 by The Lockman Foundation. Used by permission.

Printed in Canada

Print ISBN: 978-1-4866-2111-8
eBook ISBN: 978-1-4866-2112-5

Word Alive Press
119 De Baets Street, Winnipeg, MB R2J 3R9
www.wordalivepress.ca

Cataloguing in Publication may be obtained through Library and Archives Canada

Contents

Getting Started

Psalm 34:14b: "... *seek peace and pursue it.*" This concept startled me early in my adult Christian walk. I'd always felt that peace was something I could just "slide into" with a little more self-control, but the psalmist jarred my half-heartedness and I was set on a quest to "seek" peace and "pursue it." Little did I realize that this would involve a major house-cleaning of the heart and many lessons on submission and trust. I discovered that the descriptions and meanings for peace were numerous: a state of tranquility or quiet; freedom from agitation or war either internally or externally; freedom from fear, anger, anxiety; calmness and rest; harmony and reconciliation; order.[1] However, the most comprehensive biblical concept of peace rests heavily on the Old Testament "shalom," which means completeness, soundness, wholeness, and right relationship. While it includes the full list of attributes in "tranquility" of spirit, it is unshakeable, undisturbed by circumstance.

In practical terms, peace means more than resting by a gentle stream, viewing a magnificent tropical sunset, or celebrating children that never argue. Although these are often a special kiss from above, God's amazing peace is an anchor when that same stream becomes a raging river, black clouds threaten on the horizon, and sibling tempers flare.

When we repent and respond in faith to Jesus, He saves us, and peace is born (Romans 5:1). Peace is found in His presence—it steadies the heart so that we can hear God in the impending storm. It maximizes relationships, minimizes regrettable reactions, and settles our anxious hearts. Being at peace

---

1 *KJV Dictionary*, s.v. "Peace," https://av1611.com/kjbp/kjv-dictionary/peace.html, accessed November 6, 2020.

helps us let go of our expectations about timeframes, trusting that God is in control. As well, we can affect atmospheres around us for the good, delivering His peace to calm and comfort the fearful, frenzied, and broken.

In this devotional, we'll take a glimpse at some Bible personalities and events that teach us about peace. As well, we'll glean from the testimonies of some incredible women of God who will share wisdom from their personal "boot camp" experiences in pursuing peace. I know you'll appreciate the honesty and vulnerability with which they recount their journeys.

It's my prayer that in these thirty days you'll be inspired to revisit the pursuit of peace in your personal growth. I pray the Holy Spirit will shine a light on some of the deeper issues that may be depleting your peace. I know this time spent with God, and with the testimonies of His work will bring a new rest to your spirit. Be sure to pray the brief prayers at the end of each reading and take a few moments to let God make any necessary adjustments so that you'll begin to walk in a new "shalom," fully apprehending His soundness, wholeness, and harmony.

A Bumpy Ride

Day One

"He said to them (His disciples), 'Let us cross over to the other side.' ... And a great windstorm arose, and the waves beat into the boat, so that it was already filling. But He was in the stern, asleep on a pillow. And they awoke Him and... He arose and rebuked the wind, and said to the sea, 'Peace, be still!' And ... there was a great calm."

—Mark 4:35b, 37–38a, 39, NKJV

The crowd was ready to disperse. Evening had come, and Jesus invited His disciples to cross over to the other side of the lake with Him. You can be sure that at that moment everything looked good from the shore—calm seas, a still evening, a gentle breeze. *"Let us cross over to the other side."* That statement was a promise from their leader that they would get there. But as with many transitions in our lives, things can look good from the dock until the unexpected, until the storm hits. The moment we pull up the anchor and leave the place of familiarity, it's like all hell breaks loose.

I heard a message by T.D. Jakes in 2014 that left me with some significant thoughts on this passage. He pointed out that people are always happy on their wedding day; business partners are overjoyed when they open the new company; and on the first day of a new job, everybody welcomes you. But you don't really know who you've married until your child contracts a serious illness. You don't know who your business partner is until the bank wants to foreclose on your company. Those welcome faces at the new job can turn hostile a few weeks in when you seem to be getting the better assignments. When the storm is raging and the waves are high, you can quickly lose your peace. You have to make decisions you didn't anticipate, and you can't put your trust in the blue sky and the gentle ripples of the clear water that you observed back on the shore.

But remember, you are with Him and He made a promise—you will get to the other side. As soon as the disciples forsook the posture of the promise, their trust in Him eroded. They asked of Jesus, who was peacefully sleeping in the boat and seemingly unaware of the bumpy ride, *"Do You not care that we are perishing?"* If you panic under the threat of the storm, you relinquish your position of trust and give room to the enemy to bring fear and anxiety. This begs the questions: Do I only trust Jesus when the weather is good? Do I still love and trust Him in the surgery, in the unemployment line, in the marital arguments? Our peace is tested when the ride is bumpy, but the storm helps to define character and proves the depth of relationship.

Jesus is the Prince of Peace, and He doesn't need any of the variables in the atmosphere to be working right in order to take charge of the situation. What is significant in this picture isn't what Jesus spoke *to* but where He spoke *from*. If you have peace on the inside and the crisis hits your circumstances, you can speak out that supernatural Holy Spirit peace from the reservoir within. You can speak what your God is able to do! Your boat will never go down because of the water around it, but if you let the things around you flood over to the inside, they will take you down for sure. Even in the bumpy rides, dwell on the promise, not the problem. You are partnered with the Prince of Peace, and He has promised that He will get you to the other side.

Jesus, I can be fearless and filled with faith when I believe the promises of your word, but I confess that I often waver in my trust when the waters are rough. Today, I choose to renew my trust in you. As I meet the unexpected, I will re-member that you are in the boat with me and you can already see the other side.

The Key to Peace

Day Two

"Let all bitterness and wrath and anger and clamor [perpetual animosity, resentment, strife, fault-finding] and slander be put away from you, along with every kind of malice [all spitefulness, verbal abuse, malevolence] . . . forgiving one another [readily and freely], just as God in Christ also forgave you."
—Ephesians 4:31, 32b, AMP

I still recall that Saturday afternoon when we got the call about my dad. He'd been rushed to the hospital after a procedure at the long-term care home. He was a man who often had trouble with a short fuse, but he had a sharp mind, a healthy body, and an active social life with his siblings. A Bible school student in his younger days, there wasn't much scriptural trivia that would stump him.

It was a two-hour drive to reach him, and he took his last breath before we arrived. The autopsy report confirmed it was a medical accident related to a procedure by an unqualified and unsupervised nursing personnel. The news was devastating. Though in disbelief, my brothers and I felt that someone must take responsibility for this sudden and avoidable loss, and something must ease the pain of this senseless, negligent behaviour. We had all the ammunition needed for the courtroom and every chance of winning a case.

I found myself filled with confusion and disbelief and asking why. I was in a fight, and I recognized it wasn't the good fight. I found myself joining forces with revenge, anger, hatred, and oppression. Peace eluded me. I was hating the wrong things—people! Hebrews 12:14 says to pursue peace with all people. I had to answer a hard question: Was my time to be invested in pursuing justice for my dad as I saw it, or in pursuing Him, the Prince of Peace?

God's comfort, the outflow of His peace nature, was my greatest need. I couldn't initiate a right and godly response in my own strength, but wrapped in His comfort, with His help, I could make the conscious choice to give the gift of forgiveness. He helped me to release to Him the things I couldn't and still don't understand. Finding peace meant letting go! I wasn't saying it was okay—I was just saying, "God, you take it from here."

No one from that long-term care home ever offered an apology, but I learned that I have the power to choose to forgive, whether or not the other person acknowledges what they did, feels sorry about it, or changes their ways. I had so much to gain by letting it go: true inner peace, an ability to worship with a clear conscience, freedom, and ready access to my Saviour. A court battle and a financial settlement, revenge, and public shaming of the offenders could never buy any of those. It's what God required of me, and it changed everything within. F. B. Meyer said, "As we pour out our bitterness, God pours in his peace."[2] As I forgave, I found that I was no longer tormented by the memory of this hurt or by the emotions it evoked in me initially.

The Greek word that translates to "forgiveness" literally means "to let go," as when a person doesn't demand payment for a debt. Many people have done things to us and to people we love, and they cannot pay for it—there's no possible way they can repair the damage they've done or replace what they've taken or destroyed. The Bible teaches that unselfish love is the basis for true forgiveness, since love *"keeps no record of wrongs"* (I Corinthians 13:5b). Forgiveness opened my pathway to peace, and that peace grows greater day by day.

Holy Spirit, sometimes it's hard to let go, but today I'm choosing the high road that keeps me intimately connected to my heavenly Father. I choose to forgive. Pour your healing into the wounds and, as I gain my freedom, teach me how to walk in both wisdom and love in the days ahead.

2   "85 Quotes about Peace," *Christian Quotes*, accessed September 16, 2020, https://www.christianquotes.info/quotes-by-topic/quotes-about-peace/

Transforming Peace

Day Three

Contributed by Janet Soppitt

"God makes his people strong. God gives his people peace."
—Psalm 29:11, MSG

After moving to Canada, my husband, five children, and I encountered many challenges. We struggled with adjusting culturally, found it hard to make ends meet financially, endured much sickness in the family as our bodies acclimatized to new environments, faced the sudden loss of my father, and struggled to pastor a broken and hurting church. Over time, the accumulation of all these stressors significantly affected my husband and he became sick with depression and anxiety. It was only after three years that he was eventually diagnosed with bipolar 2, and while he was mostly depressed, he began to improve with the help of medication. His illness continued for seven years and included many periods of hospitalization when I had to care for him and our struggling family as well as find work to support us. It was a long, intense time of relentless challenge and pressure.

In the course of learning how to care for someone who was struggling with mental health issues, I learned that during this time, you're 50 per cent more likely to succumb to depression yourself, and I often felt as if I was teetering on the edge of this, having to fight to choose to believe that God really was good and was for us rather than against us—contrary to what all of our circumstances seemed to suggest. Many times I felt as if I couldn't go on anymore, and I would cry out to God for help. My journals from those years were peppered with such entries as I poured out my heart to the only one who could save us, while wondering if He would.

On one such occasion on a Sunday morning, I was feeling extremely low and hopeless. I cried out to God for some encouragement, telling Him that I was afraid I was suffering from depression myself and was fearful of what would become of us as a family if I couldn't work. I picked up my Bible and it fell open at Psalm 46. As I read the familiar verses about calamity and destruction, which completely mirrored how I felt about our home, I was powerfully struck by verse five, which said, *"God is within her, she will not fall …"* It was as if God had come into the room, lifted my heaviness, reminded me of who He is, and instantly filled my heart with peace and joy, giving me courage, confidence, and strength for the next leg of the journey.

Encounters like this, though not everyday occurrences, were certainly not out of the ordinary. Over a period of fifteen years of chaos and confusion, each time God revealed Himself to me in my darkness, I gradually began to see life differently and learned to live out of the peace that passes understanding. I'm not quite sure how it happened, but it was a gradual process of transformation during which I learned to lean into the one who is able and faithful to do what He has promised. And the good news is that this peace is accessible to all of us as we draw near to Him; in fact, not only is it available, but He delights to impart it to us.

Jesus, you are my rock and my salvation. In the deepest and darkest moments when I feel hopeless and overwhelmed, you remind me that you are still my foundation. You become strength in my weakness and encourage me with your words of truth. Thank you for the peace I find in your presence.

The Peacemaker

Day Four

"Blessed are the peacemakers, for they will be called children of God."
—Matthew 5:9

We don't always have to get our own way in order to solve a conflict. In fact, the quicker we're willing to step back and refuse to die on every hill, the quicker many situations can be resolved. We can learn a lot from men and women in the Bible by watching the choices they made and the resulting consequences.

Abraham and Lot, who had travelled together since Ur, found themselves in Canaan in a tense and problematic situation, and some choices had to be made. This scene is set in Genesis 13, where it's recorded that a conflict arose between the two men. They both had been blessed with more than they needed, and each of them possessed many flocks, herds, and tents. Their abundance of animals had put a strain on the land and caused strife between the two groups of herdsmen. In fact, it caused such a problem that they realized they would need to divide camp in order to provide ample grazing area for the plenitude of animals, but all the land had actually been promised to Abraham.

Abraham knew it would be better to not be with Lot than to be at odds with him. Abraham wanted to keep peace in the family while ensuring that Lot would find sufficient vegetation to feed his animals. He wasn't going to send his nephew back to Haran. Led by his generous and conciliatory heart, and his trust in God, Abraham decided to give Lot any piece of land he selected in order to be at peace in the relationship. He was willing to step back, as he didn't desire to make this a battle. Abraham trusted that God would make good on His promises, and he didn't feel the need to fight with Lot for what he preferred. What a great picture of contentment and trust! Abraham refused to allow possessions to become a priority over his love for a person. The luscious plain of the Jordan Valley drew Lot's attention. He saw what was before his eyes (without seeing the wickedness of Sodom and the future consequences of his choice) and he chose according to his own best interests. Abraham served God as a peacemaker in what could have become a nasty situation with his nephew. They were family. He took initiative to mend relations.

"One of the greatest examples of humility in action is to act as a peacemaker in conflict involving ourselves."[3] At times we worry too much about being taken advantage of, or not standing up for what is rightfully ours, and we lose sight of how our "me first" actions might affect a valued relationship. Sometimes we get what we want, but in the process we hurt people, distance people, and lose close relationships.

While peacemaking doesn't consist of ignoring a problem, or simply appeasing a bully, it does sometimes mean laying down the sword and giving more than what's required. As Jesus said, "Go the extra mile" (Matthew 5:41). This incident in Abraham's journey reminds us that one of the best ways to deal with strife and relieve quarrels is to take the initiative to be the peacemaker.

This chapter begins and ends with Abraham worshipping God. It shows that his heart is fully fixed on God. Peacemaking is a divine work. God is the author of peace, and Jesus is the supreme peacemaker. Consider serving Him today as the peacemaker that your family, your friends, your workplace, and your world so desperately need. As you trust God and look to Him, you'll find contentment within and greater peace and joy in your relationships.

Lord, make me an instrument of your peace. Help me to set aside selfish desires that are hurting relationships. Help me to go the extra mile.

---

3   Jerry Bridges, "What Does It Mean to Be a Peacemaker?" *Outreach Magazine*, accessed September 22, 2020, https://outreachmagazine.com/resources/17672-what-does-it-mean-to-be-a-peacemaker.html.

Peace in Loss

Day Five
Contributed by Marion Venables

"Let the morning bring me word of your unfailing love, for I have put my trust in you. Show me the way I should go, for to you I entrust my life."

—Psalm 143:8

Just thirteen days earlier our new congregation was congratulating us on the birth of twin granddaughters. We were joyous for our son, Peter, and his wife, Louise. Now on the day before our son's birthday, we were receiving sympathy messages because one of his twin girls had died from complications. We had seen these precious, tiny, fragile babies in their individual incubators, and we had such hope for them. The identical girls had been born at twenty-four weeks and weighed 2 and 2.1 pounds— not insurmountable for many twins born that early, but for Samantha it was.

This sorrow was compounded by the fact that only ten months earlier, Peter and Louise had also suffered the stillbirth of their first child, a boy named Jared. That alone had been a great sorrow. Two babies in ten months was devastating and unthinkable. Who can understand such things? We are pleased, of course, for those who have healthy babies; however, when immersed in sorrow at the loss of your child, it seems unfair. Often when I see twins, even today, I feel a twinge of pain.

I have learned that life may not be fair, but God is. God is love. He doesn't dispense death and disease on His children, no matter what age. In fact, He promises that He will be with us through every painful moment. I have known people who experience profound pain almost every hour of every day, and they credit the presence of God with being their sustenance. Our God is there to give the strength and courage to endure.

We were honoured to conduct the service for this little girl of ours. Our new church family was so kind, loving, and supportive in every way. As pastors trying to minister to our family and Louise's family during this time, we failed to make time for our own personal process of grieving. Weeks later, when the grief hit us full force, we knew we needed to face our pain and sorrow and the ache within over the loss of this precious granddaughter we never got to hold. We needed to bring it to our heavenly Father and embrace His unfailing love. I love the phrase "unfailing love," found so often in the Psalms. It is God's all-embracing eternal love that leads us through each day, beginning to end, and through every situation in life.

Today, the surviving twin, Allison, is seventeen and in Grade Twelve. She has a younger sister, Gwyn. Though thirteen-and-a-half months separate them, they grew up acting more like twins than just sisters. Every year on October 6, Louise posts a reflective poem on Facebook to express her love for the baby she held only on the day she died.

Facing the death of someone you love—a child, spouse, parent, close friend—is one of life's most difficult experiences. Death shakes us to the core, whether the shaking is immediate or delayed. In those moments, as believers we draw near to our powerful and loving heavenly Father, who not only stands beside us but lives within us! His presence makes it impossible for us to be alone in that moment of pain. He said, *"Peace I leave with you; my peace I give you. I do not give to you as the world gives"* (John 14:27a). We proved His Word to be true. He is near to the broken-hearted with a unique, promised nearness and peace that only He can provide. He is the God of unfailing love.

Holy Spirit, I'm so glad that in the most difficult of moments, you pray for me with groanings that cannot be expressed in words (Romans 8:26b). Thank you for the strength we find in one another in our times of shaking. You are my source of joy, and I will not weep forever (Psalm 30:5). Your presence is my peace, and I am sustained by your unfailing love.

Living Today with My Shepherd

Day Six

Psalm 23

Their sweet, cherished grandma was getting weaker and Heaven seemed closer. The family had called me to help prepare for an imminent celebration of her life. As we sat down with her Bible to search for a suitable passage, we saw that many pages were loose and multiple verses were underlined, highlighted, and barely legible for the years of marking. The earmarked leaves of that Bible contained a record of those prayed for by name and were marked with dates and prayers. Psalm 23 had been torn and taped—obviously it had been an anchor to Grandma through the many seasons of her well-lived life.

As I sat at Grandma's bedside during that night, her treasured Bible on my lap, it became clear to me that this psalm of David, though often a favourite for the end of life journey, had been for her a psalm for living. In this psalm, using skillfully chosen images, David shared his testimony, his personal experience with God. Beneath the beauty of his words were solid convictions formed in the crucible of crisis.

I began to see Psalm 23 as a journey, a pilgrimage. The fields, the valleys, the rod, and the staff would all be found at some point on the pages of the story of David's life. In the flesh, he was a shepherd who cared for his sheep, but he knew the security, safety, and reassurance of *the* shepherd with whom he had a deep relationship. It was the shepherd who set the pathway. Without his direction, the sheep would be lost and alone, subject to the attacks of enemies, the elements, and disease. Life was in jeopardy unless the shepherd was alert and attentive.

The shepherd could only reach higher ground by climbing up through the valleys with sides scarred by deep ravines. Every valley was a pathway to something better, but in those valleys there was always present the prospect of death. The genuine peace David expressed was a peace that could only come from trusting God deeply. He had experienced Him as *"my shepherd"* (Psalm 23:1). The peace was built on the promise of His presence.

He leads us beside still waters—the quiet place where we drink in His peaceful presence. David reiterated God's devotion to refresh and restore when the struggles of the journey deplete our vitality. God does some of His greatest work when we rest.

David also noted that *"You prepare a table before me in the presence of my enemies. You anoint my head with oil; my cup overflows"* (Psalm 23:5). It would make more sense to the natural mind that a "good" shepherd would just keep the sheep away from enemies, but God's ways are beyond understanding. He doesn't ask us to wait until the impending attack and hostility has passed and the battle is finished to sit at His table.

David was supremely confident not only about his present circumstances, but in God's faithfulness for the future. He could say not just "perhaps" or "possibly," but that "surely" (with assurance) goodness and mercy would follow him all the days of his life, and he knew he would dwell in the house of the Lord forever (Psalm 23:6). He found life well worth living, and he delighted in the ultimate peace … dwelling in God's presence.

I think Grandma's cup overflowed from that fragile page of her Bible that night, providing a relevant and powerful message for those who would soon celebrate her life. Grandma knew that this peace wasn't just to be stored away for the future but was something she chose to experience every day. Think of it—His presence right now in our day-to-day lives, anytime, anywhere. We can safely follow the Good Shepherd as we wend our way through life's journey.

> *Lord, today I confess that I need you as my shepherd. I need your provision, your presence, your protection, and your peace. I invite your anointing to minister new life to my spirit today.*

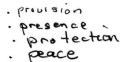

" P's "
. prouision
. presence
. protection
. peace

Peace at Its Source

Day Seven
Contributed by Abby Clattenburg

"Do not be anxious about anything, but in every situation, by prayer and petition, with thanksgiving, present your requests to God. And the peace of God, which transcends all understanding, will guard your hearts and your minds in Christ Jesus."

—Philippians 4:6–7

Being newly married is such an exciting and monumental season in life. There are many "firsts" to navigate as a team. While the majority of these are full of joy and fun, there are also times that can feel trying and low. Highs and lows, curves and detours, successes and celebrations—all would seem normal and anticipated, but nothing could have helped us predict or imagine the unforeseen challenges we would encounter. It might be best described as a lot of unexpected chaos!

These trying moments tested my peace. At times I felt myself overcome with anxiety and impatience. My ability to be the energetic, creative, supportive, and attentive contributor I'd hoped to be was interrupted by a concussion caused by a fall. Many of my personal dreams and pursuits had to be set on a shelf temporarily, as the healing took much longer than anticipated. One night as I was praying, I felt God whisper to my heart that I had let my outward circumstances fill me and steal my peace. Peace is a promise that we gather from God many times in scripture, but it's our personal choice whether we choose His peace or not.

Many times in my marriage I looked to my circumstances to change, or for my husband to provide my peace. I sacrificed peace in my own life because I had misplaced my source, but peace can't be perfected in us from any other source than the Lord. Every other person or thing that we try to fill ourselves with other than God is broken and temporary, leaving us to feel that peace is situational rather than unchanging. The expectation for what marriage should look like according to 1 Corinthians 13, if misunderstood, can mark our spouse as our source of perfect love: "My husband is patient; my husband is kind. My husband does not envy ... he is not easily angered; he keeps no record of my wrongs ... He always protects, always trusts ... and definitely should never fail (to be whatever I need)!" But the only perfect source of each of those qualities is the Lord. He knows us inside and out and has perfect plans for us. He's working things together for the good of those who love him.

I started gaining my peace back in marriage when I started looking for God to be the source of my needs. His fullness and perfection give us a peace that can't compare. When I worked to fill myself with God—body, mind, and spirit—I was able to more selflessly attempt to love my husband better, even while working on the 1 Corinthians 13 expressions of love. I placed my hopes in the Lord rather than on my husband, and that gave us both more grace in loving one another. Peace isn't the absence of conflict in our lives— it's the presence of the Lord. When we choose to invite Him into our lives, our circumstances, and our marriages, He will bring His peace.

Circumstances will change, but the Lord is unchanging, and His invariable, abiding presence has been here to bring me peace as I've navigated being on a healing journey and being a newlywed. I challenge you to choose peace with God and your spouse. Invite the Holy Spirit into your lives, situations, and communication with one another. Make it a goal to create a space with God independently and together to fill yourselves with more of His perfection, and His peace will follow your pursuit of Him.

Come, Holy Spirit, breathe into my chaos and fill me with your peace. When my pain and frustration bring me to tears, quiet me in your love. Forgive me for the times I've held others hostage to expectations that only you can fulfil. Help me to embrace my true source of strength and wholeness.

The Prince of Peace

Day Eight

"For unto us a Child is born, unto us a Son is given ... And His name will be called Wonderful, Counselor, Mighty God, Everlasting Father, Prince of Peace. Of the increase of His government and peace There will be no end ..."
—Isaiah 9:6–7a, NKJV

For unto us—peace! Peace is also a person. Tucked into the familiar Christmas narrative in Luke 2:13–14, we read that some shocked and fearful shepherds spending a tiresome and routine night in a field with their sheep were visited by an angel: *"And suddenly there was with the angel a multitude of the heavenly host praising God and saying: 'Glory to God in the highest, and on earth peace, goodwill toward men!"* (NKJV).

Notice that the peace is *on* earth but not *from* earth or *of* earth. What preceded this sudden excitement and the massive assembly of praise about this coming peace? In verse twelve, we find the clue, the sign that would confirm to the shepherds that Heaven has spoken: *"And this will be the sign to you: You will find a Babe wrapped in swaddling cloths, lying in a manger"* (NKJV). Immediately following these words, the multitude of angels made their entry, joining that single angelic heavenly broadcaster. God's glory and man's peace rested in that lowly manger. Peace had come, and it would reside in the hearts of those who would receive the gift.

He left His throne, came as an infant, and rested in an unpretentious feeding trough. On that special night, something marvellous became available to all of mankind. It wasn't an earthly peace, but it was an embodied peace, the peace *of* God that made available peace *with* God for all of us. In the words of an old hymn by Peter Bilhorn, "Sweet Peace, the Gift of God's Love":

> There comes to my heart one sweet strain,
> A glad and a joyous refrain,
> I sing it again and again,
> Sweet peace, the gift of God's love.
> Peace, peace, sweet peace,
> Wonderful gift from above;
> O wonderful, wonderful peace,
> Sweet peace, the gift of God's love.[4]

The path for Jesus that ensured our peace would some day lead Him to Gethsemane and to a hill where He would die on a cross at the hands of sinful men. He was the perfect, sinless one who would make possible our peace with God, but He would walk this earth and be subject to ridicule, betrayal, pain, and misunderstanding. The Passion Translation explains it this way: "*Our faith in Jesus transfers God's righteousness to us … This means we can now enjoy true and lasting peace with God, all because of what our Lord Jesus, the Anointed One, has done for us*" (Romans 5:1). God sent his son, the Captain of the Lord of Hosts, the destroyer of the works of the enemy, and our peace.

I love this declaration from Romans 15:13: "*Now may the God of hope fill you with all joy and peace in believing, that you may abound in hope by the power of the Holy Spirit*" (NKJV). How will I experience joy and peace from the God of hope? What connects me to God and His peace? It's in the believing and receiving! This peace is from God, and it comes through Christ, the Prince of Peace. If we truly desire peace, we must find it in believing and receiving the gift of Jesus. May I encourage you today to revisit the manger and see for yourself.

> *O God, I'm forever grateful that I can enjoy true and lasting peace with you through Jesus, the Prince of Peace. I join in praise with the angelic host as I am reminded to revisit the manger. Teach me to live life to the full, experiencing your unending peace and abounding love.*

---

4   Peter B. Billhorn, "Sweet Peace, the Gift of God's Love," *Hymnary.org*, accessed November 23, 2020, https://hymnary.org/text/there_comes_to_my_heart_one_sweet_strain.s

We revisit the manger and realize that this gift when believed & received is a result of the cross.

Depleted but not Departed

Day Nine

"'Though the mountains be shaken and the hills be removed, yet my unfailing love for you will not be shaken nor my covenant of peace be removed,' says the Lord, who has compassion on you."

—Isaiah 54:10

"Stop it, all of you, right now! Can't I get five minutes of peace around here?" The words of my mom—all 4 feet 11 1/2 inches of her. When she said it, we knew she meant it, but we were also aware that there were four of us and only one of her. We had the advantage, and we never let that slide by.

My three rambunctious younger brothers could drum up more disasters in a day than most families could in a year. It was never beyond them to create projects that were illegal, dangerous, or uniquely preposterous. After my petite, helpless mom had to deal with her boys spray painting the family car red while Dad was at work, clearing the local grocery store of all their seed packets, or using all of our mattresses to construct a community trampoline, she was well deserving of some peace!

Upon becoming a mother, I developed a few key phrases of my own that expressed a similar frustration. Raising three and fostering 131 (short or long term) children over the years gave me ample opportunity to plead for peace: "All right, everyone outside in the yard to play for twenty minutes. I'm locking the door, and no one can knock unless someone's bleeding." That was definitely a favourite.

There will always be circumstances that can deplete our "peace reservoirs," but if we can be alert to the ones with which the enemy targets us persistently, we can learn to access the peace that is already ours through the Holy Spirit. My "peace drainers" that go beyond the irritation of rowdy children include:

- Being in a disagreement with someone without making things right: My thought life is not at rest. I'm frustrated, guilt-burdened, and angry. And my peace is depleted.
- Busyness and rushing: The "I have to hurry" voice in my head must be re-programmed at times to take a back seat to quietness and moments in His presence.
- ⊙ Regrets and stupid mistakes: I have to remind myself that there are things I can't go back and change, and I have to leave them at the cross. A good dose of God's love will expel both shame and regret. They cannot become my identity.
- Times when my mind, will, and emotions are at war, each one fighting for the privilege to be in control: To access peace, I have to send my emotions to the back of the train, get my will aligned with God's, and look for any lies that my mind is believing. This means making sure the Spirit is in the engine room.
- Second-hand offences: It's challenging to remain at peace when someone close to me has been treated unjustly, but there are just too many conflicts in life to fight them all. To maintain or grow my peace, I have to genuinely care, do what's right in the situation, and trust in the power of prayer.

If you find your peace being syphoned off, it's time to take inventory. Think about what or who has depleted your peace and engage in a conversation with your heavenly Father so that peace can be restored. Repent for your part in opening any door to fear, anger, or judgement. Discover the lies you're believing about God, yourself, or others and put those lies to death at the cross. Your list will be very personal. Peace can become a priority for you, and your reservoir will continue to fill and overflow.

✳ *Lord, today I pray that you would reveal to me the "peace drainers" in my life. Thank you for your covenant of peace that holds strong even when I feel depleted. You are the one who refreshes and restores and brings me peace.*

To keep peace during troubling times remember the faithfulness of God. God is your source.
James 1:17 - God is the source of peace.
Every good & perfect gift,

The Renewed Mind:
Reprogrammed for Peace

Day Ten

"For the mind-set of the flesh is death, but the mind-set controlled by the Spirit finds life and peace."

—Romans 8:6, TPT

There are several computer programmers in our family. I've been fascinated repeatedly by the work in which my son-in-law, Justin, engages. Most of his recent assignments as the Canadian executive of his work organization have taken him to airports across Canada—Gander, Winnipeg, Iqaluit, Fort Nelson, and more. As a programmer, Justin says that it's the end user of the software who needs to be able to use it with ease. He explained that just as spoken English is a language, the programming language facilitates the outcome. It must be written with accuracy and without errors, or the results will be undesirable and sometimes chaotic. There's a testing time where any faulty language must be debugged by searching for and correcting wrong commands, and once the program is correct, you'll see the desired results.

In the case of our natural mind, we're often programmed by past experiences, people's words, events, circumstances, and beliefs in such a way that our thinking needs to be debugged. The scriptures describe this in Romans 12:2 as a renewing of our minds. This is God's way of saying to do some testing and be sure that what we're thinking is correct, based on His truth.

If our thoughts don't line up with God's Word, He has left us instructions on how to renew or reprogram: "*We use our powerful God-tools for smashing warped philosophies, tearing down barriers erected against the truth of God, fitting every loose* thought and emotion and impulse into the structure of life shaped by Christ" (2 Corinthians 10:4–5, MSG).

A second set of instructions is found in Philippians 4:8: "*Finally … whatever is true, whatever is noble, whatever is right, whatever is pure, whatever is lovely, whatever is admirable—if anything is excellent or praiseworthy—think about such things.*" This truth will help us displace the language of fear, discouragement, resentment, lust, insecurity, or anger. We need the source of truth to help us change.

As with Justin's computer languages, replacing wrong thoughts with God's thoughts requires attention, diligence, and accuracy. God has designed weapons for our victory. When we use His weapons, we can tear down strongholds, stand firm in Him, and have peace of mind. Wrong thinking doesn't need to defeat us. We can deprive harmful thoughts of their power and their ability to control us. Sometimes we're simply guilty of entertaining thoughts that should have been just momentary. We allow them to feel at home; we feed them, and they settle in more deeply. Lies become programmed into our thinking, and we cease to have the peace that truth can bring.

as a man thinks, so is he

Maybe you've even found yourself entertaining thoughts like, *I'm such an idiot; This is hopeless; I'll probably lose this job, just like I did the last one.* If so, you'll *Take no thought saying* likely find yourself coming up short on peace. These thoughts don't pass the test of worthy, true, or praiseworthy. Ask the Holy Spirit, who will guide you in all truth (John 16:13), what Heaven says. Renew your mind with the truth of His Word: I am God's workmanship (Ephesians 2:10); I can do all things through Christ who strengthens me (Philippians 4:13); He has plans for me that include a future and a hope (Jeremiah 29:11). *amen!*

For the Christian, our goal is abundant life in which we experience His peace and joy. Perhaps it's time for a little testing—debug with the Word of truth, welcome some new patterns of thought, and enjoy a new and settled peace.

2 Cor 10:4-5 .. "Casting down imaginations"... winging into captivity every thought to obedience of Christ",

Heavenly Father, I invite you to run whatever tests are needed to set my mind on truth and promise. As I learn to replace those wrong thoughts, help me to build a new life-giving pattern shaped by you. Remind me that the answers I need are found in your Word and not in in the world. Guide me with your peace to my future and my hope.

Eph 5:26 .... cleansed her by the washing of water with the Word.

When Peace Eludes

Day Eleven

Contributed by Stephanie Courtney

"Return to your rest, my soul, for the Lord has been good to you."
—Psalm 116:7

It was a cool day in the autumn of 2019 when the Lord brought this scripture to life in my spirit. As a wife and stay-at home-mom to four kids, I spend a good deal of my time in the kitchen. I was preparing dinner that day when my audio Bible read this portion of Psalms aloud. Tears immediately sprung to my eyes and I grabbed for a paper and pen to write it down. A few days prior, I'd experienced a battle with mental illness like never before, and it shook me to my core. This verse was God's Word spoken straight to my heart.

Before my late thirties, I'd only experienced normal anxiety. While others in my family have struggled with mental health issues, I've always been an even-keeled kind of person and figured I'd never have to grapple with it. When anxiety showed up in my life and I finally figured out what I was facing, I was admittedly blindsided. It may sound dramatic, but I didn't feel like I was the same person anymore, and I recall crying on and off for days. I grieved the loss of who I thought I was. My trust in Christ never once wavered, but I'll admit that peace felt elusive. I thank the Lord for a godly spouse and believing family members who faithfully reminded me of the peace and goodness of God.

The peace that the world offers is circumstantial. It says, "If all is right in my world, then I can be at peace." The peace that Jesus offers doesn't work like that. His peace is available when everything around us is not okay. Jesus, knowing that His disciples would be devastated by His earthly departure, spoke of peace. He said, *"my peace I give to you"* (John 14:27, emphasis added). The peace Jesus had was based on His relationship with His heavenly Father, in whom He had complete trust. This is the peace Jesus offers His followers today. It's the result of our confidence in God's goodness and our faith that His purposes will be accomplished in and through us, no matter what life throws our way.

I praise the Lord that I don't contend with anxiety daily and that with His help I'm learning how to navigate it in healthy ways when it resurfaces. When life's battles flood in and threaten to overtake us, we can remind our souls, like the psalmist did, to return to their peaceful place of rest, for God has been good and He is faithful.

Jesus, you are my safe place, my rock, my rest. You always understand me, and to think that you are mindful of me sometimes overwhelms me. You made me. You love me. Meet me where I am in this moment. You knew I'd be here. Wrap yourself around me when I'm churning inside, and quiet my spinning mind. I'm choosing to trust you today as you help me to navigate the hidden curves and the deep valleys. Thank you for ordering my steps and bringing me fresh hope in your love and goodness every day.

The Power of a Settled Heart

Day Twelve

"I have told you these things, so that in me you may have peace. In this world you will have trouble. But take heart! I have overcome the world."

—John 16:33

Paul and Silas certainly had reason to be concerned. They were outsiders who had come into the city of Philippi and had crossed paths with some wealthy business owners who had quite a unique and substantial source of income—a young girl who, through an evil spirit, could interpret signs and tell fortunes. Paul had commanded a demon to come out of the girl, and once healed, she no longer had her fortune-telling abilities. As a result, the business owners' money source dried up. They dragged Paul and Silas to the town magistrates, reporting that they were practising customs unlawful to the Romans. There was no one there to read them their rights or offer a plea bargain. Their fate looked like certain death, and even the crowd joined in the attack.

Arrested, stripped, flogged, and thrown into the inner cell of the jail in stocks and chains, they were forced to await an uncertain verdict. A jailer was called to keep watch. For anyone in Paul and Silas's situation, it would have been easy to lose hope and allow despair to set in. But they refused to be paralyzed by fear and instead trusted God in His ability to hear their prayers.

"About midnight Paul and Silas were praying and singing hymns to God, and the other prisoners were listening to them" (Acts 16:25). This part of the narrative captivates and astounds me each time I read it. Two men who had, through the power of Jesus, set a young girl free had been unjustly beaten and were lacerated, bloody, swollen, bruised, and rejected. Yet they chose to pray and have a

praise service. In the midst of their dark and discomfort, with no sterile gauze to bandage their bleeding backs, surrounded by crawling creatures and blackness, they found a place of peace within that allowed their spirits to break free of their surroundings.

others see+ listen

The other prisoners listened, and as those songs rose to Heaven, an earthquake shook the prison, the doors came open, and their chains fell off—not just for Paul and Silas but all the prisoners! The jailer in charge thought the prisoners would have welcomed an escape, and since he would be held responsible, he prepared to kill himself. Instead, he and his household were led to salvation, bathed Paul and Silas's wounds, and with them enjoyed a dinner of celebration.

Miracles usually start with a mess. Sometimes we find ourselves where we don't want to be but right where we should be. Choosing prayer and praise amid the messes can only flow from a place of settled peace that guards a trusting heart. If Paul and Silas had allowed fear, anger, or complaint to be the motivation for their prayer, they would never have advanced to praise. Without the inner stillness that comes from knowing the promise of His presence, their prayers would have been cries for justice, complaints of brutality, and curses of revenge. But their testimony of radiant hope in the darkest of moments prepared the atmosphere for deliverance, salvation, and revival.

How wonderful it would be if we had the kind of attitude that releases praise as we face the trials of our life. Martin Luther King Jr. once said, "The ultimate measure of a man is not where he stands in moments of comfort and convenience, but where he stands at times of challenge and controversy."[5] Paul and Silas were the real deal. They were believers and carriers of the gospel at every bend in the road, whether they were received with joy or beaten and imprisoned. Their choice to stay the course opened the way for the manifestation of the power of God that brought freedom and salvation to many.

Heavenly Father, keep me singing in the night times. Help me to watch for and welcome your miracles in my messes. I take heart today because you have overcome the world.

---

5   "Martin Luther King, Jr. Quotes," *BrainyQuote*, accessed October 10, 2020, https://www.brainyquote.com/quotes/martin_luther_king_jr_109228

Quiet Has Come

Day Thirteen
Contributed by Sue Keddy

"They cried out to the Lord in their trouble, and he brought them out of their distress. He stilled the storm to a whisper; the waves of the sea were hushed. They were glad when he brought them to their desired haven. Let them give thanks to the Lord for his unfailing love . . ."

—Psalm 107:28–31

"Quiet has come. The terrifying chaos has been muzzled." The English translations of God's Word pen those words of Jesus like a command, but the original text suggests that what Jesus did on the Sea of Galilee was make a *declaration*. After a long day, Jesus said to His companions, "Let's go to the other side!" So they crawled into what was probably Peter's boat and pushed themselves into the waters.

Historians and archaeologists estimate that a typical fishing boat at that time was twenty-seven feet long, just a little over seven feet wide, four feet deep, and could hold up to fifteen people, which would have been the perfect size for Jesus and His crew. The Gospel of Mark tells us that there were a few boats that followed Jesus that day, and although there were many seasoned fishermen among them, none of them expected to face a storm during that eight-mile trip across the Sea of Galilee. We know this because the scriptures tell us that a great and furious squall came up. The phrase "came up," or as some translations render, "arose," is taken from the Greek word *ginomai*, which in this case describes something that happens unexpectedly, something that catches you off-guard or takes you completely by surprise.

This storm was no small storm. It was a *great* storm, or as the Greek text says, *mega*, which we've all come to understand denotes something of *massive* proportions. The word "squall" in Greek is *lalaipsi*, which means an incredibly violent, life-threatening, overpowering, terrifying, rip apart, typhoon strength kind of a windstorm. The ferocious strength of the wind turned the peaceful waters into seething, enormous, crashing waves that quickly began to fill and capsize what was supposed to be a place of safety taking them to the next destination in their adventure with Jesus.

It was a Tuesday morning. He had just taken my hand to pray when suddenly, from out of nowhere, a gale force wind seized my boat and violently drew me under the waters. My husband and greatest cheerleader for thirty-three years was in heaven, and I was still on earth.

It was a Sunday afternoon. One second all was well, and the next my broken body was being extracted by the jaws of life out of my vehicle, which had been crushed by a speeding truck. On that Tuesday morning and Sunday afternoon, Jesus *stood up* in my boat, ushered in *His* peace, and then declared to my terrified soul, "Quiet has come. The terrifying chaos has been muzzled."

May this same Jesus stand up in your typhoon today and bring sweet calm so that everyone in the other boats around you will be included in the miraculous and compelled to get to know the one who's standing in your boat.

Jesus, I lean into your peace today. I thank you for the moments in my life where "quiet has come" and you have given me an infusion of Heaven's strength and an assurance of your presence in the midst of my storm. Teach me to be one who affects the atmosphere around me for your Kingdom's sake as you calm the chaos and hold me close. I rest in your arms of safety and give thanks for your unfailing love.

Always There

Contributed by Christal Wilson

". . . You're mine. When you're in over your head, I'll be there with you. When you're in rough waters, you will not go down. When you're between a rock and a hard place, it won't be a dead end—Because I am God . . ."

—Isaiah 43:1b–3a, MSG

I did the math. I thought I had it down to a science. I've always assumed that as a young, God-fearing woman all of my life plans would simply fall into place. When I turned thirty and only a portion of my plans had really come to pass, I began to unravel. I wanted to be married (and still do); I wanted to have kids (and still do).

There were so many plans I had for myself. When these things didn't happen, I felt lost with a touch of resentment. I felt confused with a touch of fear. Ultimately, the fear and resentment surpassed the confusion and sense of loss that I was experiencing. I thought I had done everything right, yet there I was, feeling overlooked.

Then like a cloud rolling in with stormy, destructive intention, I felt it. My heart started feeling hard, and then the hardness turned to sickness, and that heart sickness turned to complete shutdown. My sense of curiosity began to wane. Thoughts went from *Will He?* to *He won't.* My outlook began to turn to one of despair, void of peace. I started to wonder if God still saw me and if He still cared. Perplexed, I focused on a sense of duty. I became a robot—doing lots but feeling numb.

I tried to read my Bible. I tried to pray; I tried to worship, but it felt like words, songs, and prayers got caught up in my throat and couldn't make the

light → reflecting - light house.

short and significant journey down to my heart. This stalemate had reached a boiling point and I desperately needed to hear God's voice in my life.

Then one day, I heard His magnificent voice. His voice, like light, pierced the dungeon where I felt bound. His love furiously barrelled down into my heart and started to shift the atmosphere. He began to speak. He spoke louder and louder, and I felt so relieved that He was there and still revealing Himself to me. Even in silence, He was with me. Even in my anxiety, despair, and disappointment, He held my broken heart. I was accosted by His unique and intentional pursuit of me. I felt suddenly aware of the immensity of His love for me. It was always there, and I was unable to see it. But when I did, I was overtaken.

If you're reading this, know that He loves you. He loves you in your brokenness, your despair, your turbulence, your disappointment, and your anxiety. His silence speaks. His love speaks a better Word, a Word that shatters the empty promises of anxiety and fear—and His love brings peace. Lift your hands where you are; lift up a song. He will show you that He has never left your side.

Though the fig tree does not bud and there are no grapes on the vines, though the olive crop fails and the fields produce no food, though there are no sheep in the pen and no cattle in the stalls, yet I will rejoice in the Lord, I will be joyful in God my Savior. (Habakkuk 3:17–18)

Heavenly Father, thank you for reminding me today that your silence is not your absence. Thank you for your faithfulness in my times of unravelling. My hard places are not dead ends. You are always with me. My heart chooses to rejoice in you as your immense love washes over me and peace is restored.

Peace and Provision

Day Fifteen

"Now may the Lord of peace Himself grant you His peace at all times and in every way . . . [to those who walk with Him, regardless of life's circumstances]."
—2 Thessalonians 3:16, AMP

It's the 1970s. We are two working parents with two young children in early elementary school, a new home, great neighbours, and lots of dreams. The stock market is a mess, economic growth is weak, and rising unemployment eventually reaches double-digits. Rising interest rates cause a calamity, and many people are priced out of their cars and homes. This is the gruesome story of the great inflation of the 1970s, which began in late 1972 and didn't end until the early 1980s.

In 1981, mortgage rates peaked at more than 20 per cent. We had a comfortable mortgage on our newly built raised bungalow in an up-and-coming young neighbourhood with a preferred school for the children. Our mortgage was up for renewal—at a rate that was almost triple what we'd signed for just five years earlier! In real numbers, based on a $200,000 mortgage at 5.29 per cent, we were paying $1,196.45/month. By renewal date, the interest rate had jumped to 21 per cent, the high back in 1981, and our monthly payment jumped to $3,378.97. . . and that's where it would remain for the next five years.

Compound the rise in mortgage rate with my husband's work—he was paid totally on commission. When carpet sales were good, we could manage with his paycheque and my part-time return to teaching. However, when people can't pay for their cars or their homes, they don't run out to re-do their flooring! I recall more than once when a two-week paycheque was under $40.

What was most incredible about that season in our lives was that there was never a lasting moment when we doubted God's provision. There were definitely times and events in our lives that brought tears, panic, and anxious thoughts in situations much less significant than this, yet somehow we walked through this particular season in a bubble of peace, being forced—gently but of necessity—to get our priorities right. It was a season in which possessions were readily sold at Saturday garage sales, and family outings were creative and cost effective. It was a time when numbers didn't add up and we knew it was miraculous provision. A few months in, we opted to sell our home and purchase a semi-detached that would fall within a more manageable budget for us, and we knew that God was ordering our steps.

Psalm 34:10b tells us, "... *those who seek the Lord shall not lack any good thing*" (NKJV). No need is too massive or too problematic for Jesus! There was a place of peace in trusting our provider and believing that He would send all that we "needed" for the abundant life He'd promised. We learned that peace was something to be treasured more than an elegant bedroom set and valued more than a collection of Hummels. It's more beautiful than decorative art pieces and, yes, more beneficial than a bountiful paycheque. God has countless, amazing ways of providing for us. To tell the unique ways He blessed us would take a volume of its own, but remember that we're talking about a God who sent manna to feed over two million Israelites who were wandering in a wilderness. He sent ravens to feed Elijah during a famine, multiplied bread and fish to feed thousands, and multiplied oil for a widow so she could support herself and her sons.

It would be challenging to enjoy the peace of God while doubting His provision. As I look back, I realize that I was learning about my responsibility to be a good steward of what He provides while receiving a fresh revelation that everything I have is a gift from Him to me. That's more than I can ask for or imagine!

Jesus, sometimes I get frazzled over the details of provision and the "what ifs?" I declare today that you are more than enough. You promise peace to all who walk with you without measuring life's circumstances in the flesh. I will seek you first, and all the things I have need of will be added on.

Trust:

More than a Mask

Day Sixteen

Contributed by Virginia Zyta

"For you will go out [from exile] with joy and be led forth [by the Lord Himself] (and his word) with peace ..."

—Isaiah 55:12a, AMP

The dreariness of that rain-soaked morning seemed to be mirrored in the faces of all those with me in the waiting room. We'd been shuttled outside when the fire alarms blared their warning and now, nerves rattled, we were back, living in this unbelievably bad movie. How had life suddenly become so complicated? Some of us were waiting for test results and some for treatments, but in every face was the anxiousness and pain of uncertainty. It seemed we were all in the same frame of mind ... but no, something was different for me. Was it His indwelling presence or His insulating work of peace? It was so evident. I felt it, like a cozy blanket on a wintry night or a steadying hand on my shoulder. It was the Prince of Peace delivering to me in that moment a peace that was truly beyond understanding.

The journey that had brought us to this moment had begun that spring after my husband and I had returned from a long and exciting travel adventure. My son Greg had experienced the beautiful gift of a stable and life-giving second marriage to a wonderful young woman named Jill. We were shocked to learn that Jill, at the age of thirty-five, had been diagnosed with breast cancer. Eight years earlier her mom had died of cancer, and her father suffered from ALS. Jill had valiantly and lovingly fought battles for others, and now she needed our support. The learning curve was horrendous—so many decisions to make, so much that required immediate action. Harvesting eggs, fertilization, cancer genes, chemotherapy, radiation, and double mastectomy were things I knew little about but were soon to become part of my regular conversations with Jill. Dependence on God became my priority.

Day after day we cried together, prayed together, and pressed through to find that place of "peace in the midst." He came alongside us at every turn. His presence and peace carried us. We had to learn to value and seek His peace over understanding. Did that mean there were no "whys" of desperation, no frustrated sobs in the night, no anger, disappointment, or grief? Certainly not! But I knew that day in that waiting room that it wasn't simply a mask with a brave face but a deepening, overwhelming sense of safety with the Prince of Peace.

For Jill, there were further complications and nine surgeries in all. She has been amazing, facing many setbacks but responding with courage and perseverance. Our connection remains strong. Jill even started a support group for those diagnosed in her age group. I couldn't be prouder of my son, who remained hopeful and supportive, nursing her and being by her side every step.

Prayer, praising when I least felt like it, and being connected to faith-filled believers have kept my foundations firm. Nothing, however, can compare to seeking His face in a quiet place and feeling His peace fill me with a confident trust that He is still in control. It isn't just a mask we wear when things are challenging—it's a person, the Prince of Peace, who keeps us secure amid life's storms.

Thank you, Jesus, that I never have to just pretend to be okay. You are faithful to fill me with a rest in my spirit that reminds me that your presence is all I need to make it through. I can truly go out with joy and be led by peace.

Making Peace with the Past

Day Seventeen

"Great peace have they which love thy law: and nothing shall offend them."
—Psalm 119:165, KJV

Joseph was the first son of Jacob by Rachel. He was raised in a "dysfunctional family" where sibling rivalry filled the household and favouritism flourished. Joseph's brothers conspired his demise and thrust him into a pit. A forced journey to Egypt followed, and life continued its rampage of abandonment, misunderstanding, accusations, false charges, prison, and injustice.

Joseph's life was wrapped in rejection, humiliation, and pain. How did he make peace with his past so that he could fulfil the plan of God for his life? Joseph's trust in God and His promises strengthened him in those many years of trial so that he could not only forgive and save his brothers, but bless them in the time of their famine.

Martin Luther King Jr. suffered loss, racial injustice, humiliation, a broken relationship, arrest, and imprisonment. His bus boycott in Alabama from December 1955 to December 1956 drew attention to racism and segregation and involved 382 days of harassment, violence, and intimidation for Montgomery's African American community.

In a sermon Martin Luther King Jr. delivered at Dexter Avenue Baptist Church in 1957, he underscored a way of life that brought him peace despite those painful attacks: "We must develop and maintain the capacity to forgive ... Forgiveness does not mean ignoring what has been done or putting a false label on an evil act … Forgiveness is a catalyst … for a new beginning. It is the lifting of a burden or the cancelling of a debt …"[6]

Corrie ten Boom, a hero of the holocaust, experienced torture, separation, death of family members, and near starvation while she and her family were imprisoned in concentration camps for hiding Jews during the German blitz across Europe in the 1940s. Corrie and her sister, Betsie, ended up in Ravensbruck concentration camp, where living conditions were brutal, hundreds of women were executed, and Betsie died of starvation.

How did Corrie come to peace with her horrifying past? What allowed to her to later travel the world bringing a message of hope and forgiveness? She knew her God and trusted His greater plan. She believed and later preached that "Forgiveness is the key that unlocks the door of resentment and the handcuffs of hatred. It is a power that breaks the chains of bitterness."[7]

We all have a past—a mixed bag of circumstances with varying percentages of healthy, life-giving relationships and events, as well as those of pain, rejection, and heartbreaking losses. Joseph, Martin Luther King Jr., and Corrie ten Boom are timeless examples whose stories have wounds. Their victories meant trusting God in the dark places as well as the bright ones, and so can ours. Trust undergirded their willingness to forgive and break the power of damaging words and actions over themselves. All three, through trust and forgiveness, made peace with their past. "Scars are beautiful when we see them as glorious reminders that we courageously survived (and forgave)."[8]

Jesus, I'm reminded that I can be chained to my past or released, through forgiveness, to pursue my destiny. The memories are painful don't have to rule me anymore. I'm giving a gift of forgiveness, not because it was okay, but because I want to walk in wholeness and freedom.

---

6   Dr. Eileen R. Borris-Dunchunstang, "Martin Luther King on Forgiveness," *Finding Forgiveness*, accessed September 26, 2020, https://findingforgiveness.blogspot.com/2009/01/martin-luther-king-on-forgiveness.html

7   Ibid.

8   Lysa TerKeurst, Twitter Post, January 31, 2016, https://twitter.com/lysaterkeurst/status/693856310220169216.

Let the Umpire Call It

"Let the peace of God rule in your hearts ... And be thankful."
—Colossians 3:15

I can't begin to count the number of times in a week that I'm caught teetering in a decision. Sometime those decisions need an immediate response, and sometimes they need some careful thought over a span of time. In all decisions, my goal is to follow the instruction of Paul in his letter to the Colossians—in everyday terms, "Let the peace of God call the shots."

I'm talking about trying to let God's supernatural peace dominate and rule each emotion and situation that confronts me. There's no worse roller-coaster ride than when I'm being rocked sideways and up and down by out-of-control emotions! Instead, I must let the peace of God rule in my heart, as Paul encourages. The word "rule" here is from the Greek word *brabeuo*, which in ancient times was used to describe the umpire or referee who judged the athletic competitions so popular in the ancient world.

An umpire is the one who determines when rules are violated and settles differences of opinion. The umpire makes the final call. In the same way, peace can rule in the controversies that rage in our hearts. When I'm trying to discern between the voice of God and the other voices that compete for my attention, I listen to see which prompting brings His peace into my heart. The peace of God becomes the umpire or referee to help me make the right and righteous call.

How does this work? Big decisions start with prayer. In my final year of full-time teaching, I was deciding whether to go straight into an early retirement, do some part-time teaching, take on a volunteer role, travel, or do some more Bible college studies. I spent time going back and forth with each idea, and I prayed. I didn't hear the voice of God on any one of the options; I didn't receive a sign or a specific prophesy. I sought counsel from friends and got differing opinions. I didn't see any definite plan, but I did feel peace on the decision to resign. It's a test of trust when the path is hidden, but I knew my steps were ordered by Him. I wasn't anxious or unnerved at the idea of not having the plan. I was at peace. God had a big surprise awaiting me that would, by an invitation, send me off on a journey to full-time local church ministry. It hadn't even been on the option list!

The quick decisions must be preceded but what I call "banked prayer deposits" that welcome the presence of God into every moment of our lives. Walking in the knowledge that you've spent time in His presence, that you trust His promises, and that you believe He is delivering the wisdom for which you have prayed, invites the Counsellor, the Prince of Peace, to weigh in and settle any dispute in your spirit quickly. It means acknowledging a response that lines up with His character, His commands, and His compassion. Peace helps me determine whether or not I'll make certain purchases while shopping, if I'll pass along a piece of information that may hurt someone's reputation, or if I'll give my "begging" kid permission to attend a certain party.

A lack of peace often tells me that the timing isn't right, God has another plan, I'm being selfish right now, He's protecting me from something, or the decision will have regretful consequences. It's that sense inside that isn't restful. If the decision isn't urgent, I like to take time to wait for clarity. Feeling pressure to decide before I'm ready is my reminder to heed the warning in Proverbs 19:2b: *"he who hurries his footsteps, errs"* (NASB). A little extra time with God (not worrying time!) can bring a fresh perspective.

Above all, Paul says, be thankful! I am not in the game alone. I need to follow the rules, be a team player, and grow in ever-increasing victories. His peace can settle the disputes within, and I can magnify and exalt Him as I learn to pursue His peace.

Dear Lord, I give you my tendency to lean on my own hurried thoughts and solutions. I welcome a new strength and wisdom, a new trust, and a new prayerful pattern that invites peace to call the shots.

When Your World
Comes Crashing Down

Day Nineteen

Contributed by Cheryl-Ann Philip

". . . There has never been the slightest doubt in my mind that the God who started this great work in you would bring it to a flourishing finish."
—Philippians 1:6, MSG

December 2012! Life was good, things were happening, and I felt an overall sense of satisfaction and accomplishment. Our group had just concluded the first-ever post-Raptors gospel concert at the Air Canada Centre. After the concert while relaxing in my hotel room, I noticed spotting in my underwear. This continued intermittently for the next six months, and each month I brushed it aside.

One day while driving with a friend, she shared her cancer experiences. The more we talked, the more I realized that her symptoms paralleled mine. I felt the Holy Spirt say, "No more excuses. Go and get checked out." A friend who was a highly qualified medical professional referred me to two gynecologists.

I made an appointment, completed the tests and procedures, and the results came back positive for uterine cancer. That day felt like the loneliest day of my life. I kept thinking, *This is surreal. It's not really happening.*

When I met with the doctor at the hospital to discuss my next steps, the consultation felt desolate, cold, and matter-of-fact. Even though he told me that the cancer was aggressive, I was given a surgery date four months away! His posture seemed to say, "Pick a number and wait your turn!"

My gynecologist was surprised when I informed her about the late surgery date, given the diagnosis. I opened my mouth and said, "If you're concerned, I need you to go to bat for me. Be my advocate!" She did… and my surgery date was moved from November to August!

On the day of my surgery, what was supposed to be a two-hour procedure turned into six and a half hours. But instead of a big ugly scar, all I had were two puncture-like incisions. My recovery was nothing short of miraculous. I found out later that my gynecologist had cancelled her clinic so that I could have the earlier surgery and had insisted on being present to assist. The hospital staff had thought I was a VIP!

God had ordered my steps and given me four committed, faith-filled women who were my constant rocks throughout the process. He cloaked me with a supernatural peace, sheltering and securing me during my tsunami.

A month later, I received a call about post-surgery treatment. I was astonished! What treatment? In an instant, I became disoriented. I struggled to rein in my swirling thoughts. I had to hold tight to the Prince of Peace in this unexpected turbulence.

I walked through the front doors of Sunnybrook Hospital's cancer wing for that appointment, overwhelmed with death and darkness. I couldn't pray, so I sang sacred songs in my mind.

After checking multiple times between me and my medical files, the doctor looked straight into my eyes and said, "No treatment." She then said she would consult with a colleague to be sure.

At the front desk, the nurse asked to set up my next appointment date. I told her there would be no next appointment. She seemed very puzzled, as if to say, "Everyone has a next appointment." I reminded myself at that moment that I was a child of God and He had this situation in hand. That evening, the doctor confirmed that I was cleared of any further appointments.

It has been seven years since my surgery, and I continue to enjoy good health. I thank Him for life every day, for preservation in the storm, and for provision. His peace was my lifeline to victory!

Jesus, you want me to experience a life lived to the full. When my circumstances tell me to be anxious and afraid, I will choose your peace. You've got me covered.

A Legacy of Peace

Day Twenty

"Peace I leave with you, My peace I give to you; not as the world gives do I give to you. Let not your heart be troubled, neither let it be afraid."

—John 14:27, NKJV

It was just hours before He'd be tortured and die, but His mind was on His followers. It is, of course, not a time to talk about trivial matters but about significant things that He'd want His closest friends, His disciples, to remember. Jesus tells His disciples that He's leaving them and that the Father will send the Holy Spirit to be with them. He will be their comforter, teacher, and helper. In sensing their troubled hearts, Jesus speaks of the gift that He is leaving for them—He calls it another kind of peace. It's a deposit for them to possess. In that moment as He speaks to His disciples, He declares a legacy for all who will follow Him.

In the New Testament, the Greek word for "peace" is *eirene*. Its primary meaning is "the absence of war," but it can also mean a peaceful attitude.[9] To understand the meaning of the word for "peace" as the disciples would have understood it, we must look at the Old Testament word, *shalōm*. The NASB Topical Index says that this *shalōm* (peace) is a personal sense of well-being, wholeness, harmony, soundness, and security through a proper relationship with God and fellow men. Shalōm is a supernatural yet experiential

---

9   G. Kittel, G. Friedrich, and G.W. Bromiley, G. W., *Theological Dictionary of the New Testament*, translation of *Theologisches Worterbuch zum Neuen Testament* (Grand Rapids, MI: W.B. Eerdmans, 1995), 207.

"well-being." It encompasses everything that makes for our highest good.[10] This is what is expressed in the Jewish greeting of "shalom."

I grew a great gratitude for the amazing gift of this legacy of supernatural peace during an unexpected ride to the Hamilton General Hospital three years ago this month. I'd been struggling with severe dizzy spells, near blackouts, and irregular heartbeats for over a year. Five different rounds of heart monitors hadn't identified the problem. That weekend I was wearing a new device that could be read by phone immediately, and the culprit was caught!

At 7:00 a.m. the phone rang: "Have you had anything to eat or drink yet today?" I hadn't. "Please report to the Hamilton General immediately for surgery for a pacemaker." I was numb, frazzled, and rushed, but by the time I was on the bed being prepped, I had opened His gift. There was gratitude that my heart, which had been "pausing" at length, would now be supported in its work. There was favour in having one of the most experienced doctors attending to my case. There was a sense of completeness, soundness, and well-being—His peace—that I could see with eyes of faith and also experience right then.

The peace that Jesus gives is independent of outward circumstances. It's that place we can run toward when everything around us turns upside down. Once we're there, we can cease from fighting and let God fight for us. The purpose of God's peace is that our heart be "well and whole."

The peace that the world offers us is the peace of escape, one that comes from the avoidance of trouble. The legacy of peace that Jesus offers us is the peace of surrender that comes from facing the struggles, giving them to Him, and knowing that His peace is protecting our heart.[11]

Jesus, today I ask that you settle my heart. So many things are out of my control, but I know you've got them covered. As I renew my trust in your goodness, return me to that place of wholeness, well-being, completeness, soundness—peace.

---

10 "Another Kind of Peace—John 14:27, *Faithlife Sermons*, accessed October 5, 2020, https://sermons.faithlife.com/sermons/44083-another-kind-of-peace-john-14.27.

11 Ibid.

Partnered with Peace

Day Twenty-One

"And the effect of righteousness will be peace, And the result of righteousness will be quietness and confident trust forever."
—Isaiah 32:17, AMP

Daniel had been appointed as the first or highest ranking of three leading men who, along with several other princes, would help King Darius govern and lead in Babylon. Daniel's excellence in both spirit and management was without fault or flaw. Stirring in the hearts of his fellow leaders was a deep-seated jealousy that set in motion a scheme devised to get rid of Daniel. In their underhanded and malicious proposal, they convinced King Darius to make a new law in which people could worship and pray only to the king. Anyone who defied the law would be thrown into a den of lions. They were aware of Daniel's committed daily prayer times and how he faithfully and single-mindedly honoured his God.

The papers for this newly hatched regulation were signed and the announcement was made. The king's anguish was obvious as he came to realize that this would target Daniel, whom he had grown to respect and value ... but he had to follow through.

Daniel committed to remain steadfast in prayer and praise to the Lord, even if it meant a likely death. Three times a day, with his windows wide open, he simply did as he'd always done. He rose above circumstance to commune with God. This was a man at peace amid the turmoil. Daniel had committed his life into the Lord's hands. For him, prayer was much more than an escape mechanism—it was a way of life. He prayed with the full assurance that God was in control and would keep His promises.

Such peace on the outside was simply the ripple of what was within. While Daniel consistently prayed, there is no record of him panicking. Scripture would indicate that Daniel did not complain to God in those prayers. He didn't curse his enemies or call out for God to rescue him. He didn't even ask for an immediate new plan. Daniel 6:10 says he prayed prayers of gratitude from a heart that was at peace, and he prayed with trust in the God who shared His secrets with him (Daniel 5).

Daniel displayed no wavering, no second guessing, no hiding his response. As he was thrown into that den of lions, he clearly chose character over comfort, and trust over fear. A stone was placed over the mouth of the den, and the king sealed it with his own signet ring and with the rings of his nobles so that Daniel's situation might not be changed. The king returned to his palace and spent a sleepless and tormented night. Darius had all the wealth and power any man could ever want, yet he found no rest. Daniel's response in that lion's den, however, changed the atmosphere and brought an inconceivable peace—it welcomed an angel who shut the lions' mouths, and peace prevailed.

What is your default response when life presses in on you? We too can learn to be committed when it's not convenient, and peaceable when people, decisions, and rules are unjust. We can even learn to be thankful during turbulence. As you reflect on the life of Daniel, ask God to help you see the value of the fruit of the Spirit in your own life—His peace. Trust His timing and His well-established reputation of faithfulness to get you through impossible situations.

Jesus, I cling to you for my support and strength. Help me to stay committed when it's not convenient and filled with your peace when I'm under attack. Teach me to commune with you out of the place of gratitude, even when circumstances are tough and decisions seem unjust. You are my defence and my strong tower.

His Word Brings Peace

Day Twenty-Two
Contributed by Judy Chiarot

"But [in fact] He has borne our griefs, and He has carried our sorrows and pains ... But He was wounded for our transgressions, He was crushed for our wickedness [our sin, our injustice, our wrongdoing];the punishment [required] for our well-being fell on Him,and by His stripes (wounds) we are healed."
—Isaiah 53:4a, 5, AMP

I was so excited when my children were born! I still remember vividly the beautiful sunrise the morning this particular child arrived, born in only twenty minutes to bless our lives and family. Always so joyful and smiling, I anticipated the close relationship we would share, just like the one I'd experienced with my own mother.

We pastored a church, so our children were PKs (pastor's kids), and we noticed that this child began to withdraw during the preteen years. Following high school and Bible school, this child further distanced due to disappointments from difficult experiences and what was perceived as unanswered prayer. While residing in a different city, this child became especially unresponsive and distant toward me. I had a sense from the Lord to simply respond with love and acceptance, free of judgement; however, the pain, sorrow, and grief over the lack of a relationship kept causing deep distress. I knew how to stand in faith on God's promises for this child, to hold fast to God's Word that my child would come back to the Lord (Jeremiah 24:7), but I yearned for the close relationship of mother and child that had slipped away. The helplessness I felt was, at times, overwhelming. I interrogated myself with numerous questions, trying to discover what I must have done wrong.

Then one day as I was reading Isaiah 53:4–5, the Lord spoke to my heart and revealed to me that *He* had already borne my *grief, sorrow,* and *pain,* as well as my sin and sickness. In the same way I believed that I was saved and healed, I needed to cast off the sorrow, pain, and grief that I'd carried daily for twenty years and allow *His peace* to be my experience concerning my child.

Webster's Dictionary brought further clarity to what the Lord was showing me:

Bear—to sustain the burden of; endured; suffer.

Endure—implies a holding up against prolonged pain, distress, etc. (This is where patience is practised.)

Grief—intense emotional suffering; acute sorrow; deep sadness; keenly distressed.

Sorrow—mental suffering caused by loss, disappointment, sadness, grief, and regret.

God's revelation through His word calmed the storm of regret, confusion, disappointment, and distress that had plagued me throughout this journey. Since then, whenever I'm tempted to venture back into that troubled stream of sorrow or pain, I remember that Jesus already bore it for me on the cross, and I choose to rest in the safety, grace, and strength of His completed work.

Scripture says in Colossians 3:15: *"Let the peace of Christ rule in your hearts ... And be thankful."* I choose to let the peace rule in my heart instead of the sorrow and pain that He has already borne for me. I choose to meet each day with a thankful heart. I am free to walk in His peace—it's not based on the circumstances, and it will no longer be buried by my need to figure things out. I am free to see the fullness of His work on the cross for me and eagerly anticipate the time when this child will discover the depth of both His limitless love and mine.

Thank you, Lord, that peace is not out of reach. Thank you for the Word of truth that is quick and powerful to my open heart. I apply the fullness of your work on the cross to every family situation today and find that place of sweet rest and unhindered faith where I can let you do your work. Help me to remain free of striving and full of hope.

Living at Peace with Yourself

*"For we are His workmanship [His own master work, a work of art], created
in Christ Jesus [reborn from above—spiritually transformed, renewed, ready to
be used] for good works, which God prepared [for us] beforehand . . ."*
—Ephesians 2:10a, AMP

The journey to knowing and believing the truth of our identity in Christ
requires a lifetime of learning. The scripture declarations collected and
distributed by Dr. Neil T. Anderson (https://ficm.org/) continue to be invalu-
able to believers who are learning to walk in truth and at peace with oneself: I
am accepted in the Beloved; I am bought with a price; I am a child of God; I am
secure; I am significant; I am God's workmanship . . . and many more.

The struggle for peace in one's identity is a real one. So much of what we
believe about ourselves comes from the words and actions of others toward us.
If, as children, we're subjected to demeaning, damaging, and toxic words and
atmospheres, we may not, without God's healing power, understand that we
are treasured and precious. On the other hand, we may have had an abundance
of affirmation but been unable to process or believe it.

One of my favourite stories about transformation and peace with oneself is the story of the "Wemmicks" in Max Lucado's charming children's
book, *You Are Special.* The story tells of a woodcarver named Eli and his wood-
en creation, Punchinello. Punchinello's world is filled with wooden people
called Wemmicks, who reward or evaluate one another with stickers. Poorly
performing and less attractive Wemmicks wear grey dotted stickers, while the
shiny, colourful, and talented Wemmicks wear gold stars. Lucado writes that

after a while of living in this environment, Punchinello "had so many dots that he didn't want to go outside. In fact, he had so many gray dots that some people would come up and give him one for no reason at all."[12]

One day, Punchinello runs into a Wemmick with no stickers at all. He is both astonished and curious. She advises him to visit his maker, Eli, in his workshop on the hill to find the answers to his "wondering." In the visit with Eli, Punchinello asks about this very unusual girl and why she has no dots or stars:

"Because she has decided what I think is more important than what they (others) think," said Eli. "The stickers only stick if they matter to you. The more you trust my love, the less you care about their stickers ... For now, just come to see me every day and let me remind you how much I care."[13]

As Punchinello begins to believe the woodcarver, his transformation begins, and his first gray sticker falls to the ground.

This is such a beautiful reminder that we must see ourselves through God's eyes. Our transformation and our ability to walk at peace with ourselves must form the basis of our acceptance in our maker. A visit with God each day will help us to deal with the dots and the stars that others bestow upon us. We are His workmanship. What He says about us will be what matters.

Let's be reminded today that our value isn't found in what others think about us or even in the ways they affirm us—whether it's our spouse, our boss, our pastor, or our neighbour. Embark on the journey to become victorious over the labels of life. Let your mind be renewed with His truth, step into His joy, and break the power of the dots and stars!

Jesus, I have been so prone to let others label me in ways that haven't been helpful. Today I've had a new glimpse of who I am in your eyes, and it's an amazing, encouraging picture. Help me to deal with the stars and dots every day so that I stay close with you and walk in assurance and peace knowing that I am loved and valued by my maker.

---

12 Max Lucado, *You Are Special* (Wheaton, IL: Crossway Books, 1997), 13.

13 Ibid., 31

Getting on Base

Day Twenty-Four
Contributed by Betty Ann Lewis

"Cast all your anxiety on him because he cares for you."

—I Peter 5:7

As the daughter of Salvation Army officers, I grew up understanding firsthand how God uses people when their lives are committed to Him. Normal life with my parents' response to God's call into Salvation Army ministry meant that we were moved to new assignments every three or four years. This always brought some excitement and curious anticipation and kept our family extremely close.

Years later, my husband and I also answered God's call to serve full time in the Salvation Army, and with four sons, we committed to go wherever He would send us. When we were given the challenge of a new appointment, we moved on. The boys were particularly excited when we were given the opportunity to do youth work, which meant that we would be at camp each summer. We were blessed to have eight years sharing God's love in this atmosphere. We felt that life was fulfilling, and God's special bonus was having the opportunity to appreciate Canada while serving God here.

Then the question came: Would we be willing to go to Germany? The assignment would be to work with the Canadian Armed Forces as a support to the troops, their families, and the chaplains. The Salvation Army had been ministering in this capacity for many years on three bases. We would run a restaurant and a gift shop in Baden, where the folks could feel a touch of home. We'd conduct an evening chapel service and be available for the families. Without hesitation, we said yes ... and then reality hit! We realized all the paperwork and preparations that were needed. We would be leaving two of our sons and my mother, who was in her eighties. We had to have many conversations, fill out a pile of documents, and set things in place for the extended family here in Canada, all while keeping the plan under wraps. The boys were great in keeping it quiet, but finding the courage and the right time to tell my mother took some serious prayer and wisdom. Finding peace in the many preparations took focus and repeated times of giving it all to Him.

My mother had varied feelings about our decision. Sending us off to Germany triggered tragic memories of loss as she recalled her brothers going to war and having one brother killed and buried in Flanders Fields. Despite this, leaning into her great faith and her love for God brought her to willingly agree that this was where we should go. Our two sons who were going with us would be going to school on the base. The two sons staying behind were going to be well looked after, so there were no excuses.

When departure day came, my brother brought together my mother and our sons who would be remaining in Canada and we shared a meal with the family in Belleville. As we headed to the airport in Trenton, my heart started to question what we were doing. How was I going to say goodbye not knowing when I'd see them again? Could I trust that they'd be okay? There were tears; my heart was pounding as we went through security, and then we saw God's smile. He knew our hearts. Security permitted the family to come through and wait with us! What a blessing! There was no time to say more goodbyes, but a settled peace came in just knowing we were doing God's will and He would look after those we left behind. I learned that His peace comes, and it remains, when I walk in obedience, cast my anxiety on Him, and learn to trust His plans for my life.

Dear Lord, sometimes the exciting opportunities you bring send me spinning. In those moments, while I know my response is in alignment with your plans for me, I invite you to calm my fears, reassure my heart, and keep me focused on you. Your ways are so much higher and far beyond my understanding, but they are good. Thank you for cheering me on to victory with your grace and favour.

Asking Myself the Right Question: Finding His Peace

Day Twenty-Five
Contributed by Vinetta Sanderson

"You will keep in perfect peace those whose minds are steadfast, because they trust in you."

—Isaiah 26:3

It was like grief. Unemployed, I felt lost and alone. Due to a restructuring decision, I had been "invited to resign" my job, leaving a fulfilling ministry and people I loved. Although I had experienced grief after the loss of my young son and later my husband, this loss felt more confusing and conflicted.

I accepted the reasoning and held no animosity, but it takes time to process and heal from every loss. My expectation was that another door would open soon, but as time passed with still no answers, direction, or clarity, unsettled feelings overwhelmed me. Fear shifted my focus from the truth of God's promises to facing the facts of my situation and experiencing His silence.

Well-meaning, caring friends began to worry for me and with me. All too frequently I was being asked the obvious question: "What are you going to do?" While I appreciated their concern, I had no answers.

I remember the pivotal day so clearly. Frustrated and fearful and standing in my kitchen, I was talking to God about it all again. One could call it praying, but it was more like venting to a friend: "I don't know … I don't know what I'm supposed to do. I don't know what's expected of me … where to turn. I don't know what you want me to do. I just don't know!"

Immediately God broke into my outburst with a response: "What *do* you know?"

That's a great question! Instantly, I began to speak the scriptures I'd committed to memory and trusted:

"… *I know whom I have believed, and am persuaded that he is able to keep that which I have committed unto him against that day*" (2 Timothy 1: 12b, KJV).

"*And we know that in all things God works for the good of those who love him, who have been called according to his purpose*" (Romans 8:28).

"*Now this I know: The Lord gives victory to his anointed. He answers him from his heavenly sanctuary with the victorious power of his right hand*" (Psalm 20:6).

"… *this I know … God is for me*" (Psalm 56:9).

With every additional scripture, peace displaced the doubts and settled my soul. I knew I was called, chosen, and loved by my heavenly Father. Declaring truth set faith in motion, and faith reinforced trust, bringing a comforting reassurance that God would be faithful as always.

Peace isn't dependent on the absence of difficulties, disruption, or disappointments. Amid my unknowns, God's promises anchored me in the certainty that He would instruct me in the way I should go, and He would advise me and watch over me (Psalms 32:8).

Walking by faith often means waiting for answers and trusting that God sees, hears, and will come through with His better plan … one day. In the desert places of life, God asks, "Will you trust me now?" After all we've been through, He asks, "Will you trust my permission, my plan, my provision, my purpose?" In seasons and stretches of uncertainty, what we hold on to will determine our strength and stability. If we hold on to the disappointments, we'll live defeated. If we hold on to the past hurts, the present pain, and potential difficulties, we'll be depressed. But when we hold firmly to the promises of God, when we know what we know, we can rest with peace of mind in what is unknown.

Lord, you have so patiently taught me to hold to your promises. When I'm uncertain and even fearful, I invite you to come by your Spirit and renew my mind with your truth, comfort my heart with your peace, and set my faith in motion so that I might find rest in you.

Peace: The Presence of Right Relationship

Day Twenty-Six

"For he himself is our peace, who has ... destroyed the barrier, the dividing wall of hostility."

—Ephesians 2:14

God was moving in big ways, and segments of the congregation were experiencing a new depth in their spiritual life that was both invigorating and painful. Friday night was prayer night at the church, an intimate little gathering of eight to twelve committed intercessors. People were hungry for God. The Friday night of which I write was unconventional and, for me, most memorable.

The congregation was, for the most part, close knit and supportive. Fellowship was sweet... well, most of it. There was this one lady—whom I'll call Patti. It seemed she made it her priority to keep me humble and irritated. The antics were frivolous and embarrassing; nonetheless, they were real and seemed to be meant to give me strife and a bad reputation. Being around her brought static to my soul.

Patti had been reporting me to the pastor over recent months, with accusations of everything from littering the piano keyboard to leaving kids' program equipment in the church kitchen. She monitored the dates of my ladies' meetings and reported the next day that I'd left the church unlocked. As it happened, the week previous I had cancelled the meeting and was never at the church. It was evident that her reports had been fabricated, but she and I never talked about it. I just heard it from the pastor, along with a chuckle and a roll of the eyes. No one else would have guessed there was an issue, but each time I ran into her, my heart sensed an impending storm and was void of peace.

On that fateful Friday, the Lord had prompted me to change up the prayer meeting format. I asked everyone to put their name on a paper and deposit it in a bowl. We would draw names and take time to pray for the person selected. The idea was well received … and then the back door opened and in walked Patti. Really? Prayer meetings had never been her thing. She enjoyed cleaning the church, straightening the kitchen, and turning off lights. We added her name to the bowl. It was the horror of all horrors when I pulled Patti's name! Why, God? Anyone else in the room could have prayed for her more meaningfully than I. A mental argument ensued, and I came up with enough positive thoughts that could smooth things over in a prayer. But God smelled a rat! I knew it was Him when the whisper hit my spiritual ear: "I have not asked you to tolerate her. I have asked you to love her."

I recognized how ready I was to pass over this nudge and just leave things as they were. God was offering me an opportunity to turn this situation around, to be a peacemaker, to hear how He felt about Patti, and to speak those words to her. But I was the victim—she didn't deserve my prayer! She needed to apologize … yes, maybe in front of the entire group! I heard it again: "I asked you to love her." My offended heart found its way to sincerity with a yes to God, and the peace was immediate. It was a new beginning, and I was able to lay the questions to rest at the cross.

That December, I took the family along to sing some carols outside Patti's little upstairs apartment. She came out with oranges and we hugged. The complaints ended. We never became close friends, but I made carolling at Patti's an annual event. At least twice yearly I would find an encouraging card with a bookmark, signed "From a Friend," randomly placed near my regular seat at church. Thanks, Patti. Peace. I love you too.

Jesus, take me past the pain of judgement, emotional turmoil, and hurt feelings so that I may walk in the incredible peace and joy to be found in doing life your way. Keep nudging me; clear my heart of anything that doesn't bring you pleasure. Thank you for the profound fresh experience of repentance and for the peace of a forgiven and a forgiving heart.

At Peace with Others

Day Twenty-Seven

"When a man's ways please the Lord, He makes even his enemies to be at peace with him."

—Proverbs 16:7, NKJV

Rick Warren has pointed out that "Four of the Ten Commandments deal with our relationship to God while the other six deal with our relationships with people. But all ten are about relationships."[14] My experience with Patti sent me on a journey in which I invited the Holy Spirit to teach me some very direct lessons in pursuing better relationships moving forward. Today I share just a few.

To live in peace with others, we must rule our tongues: "*... slander no one ... be peaceable and considerate, and always to be gentle toward everyone*" (Titus 3:2). Our talk must aim at resolution, not simply defence. Only the Holy Spirit can produce the real fruit of peace that's needed when it comes to handling conflicts with others: "*... My grace is sufficient for you, for my power is made perfect in weakness*" (2 Corinthians 12:9a). Allowing our emotions to lead us will inevitably bypass peace.

We must become well-practised, caring listeners: "*... take note of this: Everyone should be quick to listen, slow to speak and slow to become angry*" (James 1:19). To work things out and stay at peace with another, it's best to do more listening. Seek to understand and not just to be understood. Consider becoming someone else's "safe" place.

---

14 "51 Quotes about Relationships," *Christian Quotes*, accessed November 1, 2020, https://www.christianquotes.info/quotes-by-topic/quotes-about-relationships/

We need to serve out heavy portions of forgiveness. If we want to cultivate a lifestyle of peace, we must do our best to resolve conflict with others and refuse to carry offence and unforgiveness. This is also imperative if we want to be in a right relationship with God. Be okay with giving up the right to be right, for the sake of relationship. Learn to forgive others before they even ask for it.

Kick fear and suspicion to the curb. *"Do not be anxious about anything..."* (Philippians 4:6). We need to examine honestly what receives our time and attention in our thoughts. When we live at peace with others, our consciences are free of guilt, and our minds are free of suspicion. When we walk in love, we are above suspicion. That doesn't mean we neglect discernment, allow evil to triumph, or stop praying. It means we no longer allow suspicion to control us.

Make allowances. *"Make allowance for each other's faults, and forgive anyone who offends you"* (Colossians 3:13a, NLT). Understand that everyone doesn't have to think like us, act like us, or have the same opinion as us. Sometimes they've just had a bad hair day, and sometimes they have reasons for grumpiness. Make allowances. Not everything they're doing and saying has to do with us. Be gracious, bite your tongue, and move on.

Search for the good in others: *"... in humility value others above yourselves"* (Philippians 2:3bb). Everyone is special to God. You don't have a monopoly on His love. You are unique, anointed, valued, and accepted. Try to see others from God's perspective, full of potential, deeply loved, and definitely not dispensable.

This journey to live at peace with others remains unpredictable and glaringly suspect in the flesh, but it's definitely doable in the Spirit! We can build relationships that are rewarding. Heaven's intention is that we experience the kind of unity that commands the blessing of God. That's my goal, and I've learned that healthy, life-giving relationships are one of the greatest joys of life.

Jesus, I confess that I've not always been co-operative with the Holy Spirit in giving attention to challenging relationships. Help me to think more about others and less about myself. Show me who you are asking me to make peace with to-day—and give me the wisdom to do it in love.

Let Peace Prevail

Day Twenty-Eight
Contributed by Karla Stoffelsen

"Do not be anxious about anything, but in everything by prayer and supplication with thanksgiving let your requests be made known to God. And the peace of God, which surpasses all understanding, will guard your hearts and your minds in Christ Jesus."

—Philippians 4:6–7, ESV

I grew up in El Salvador during the civil war. My family was held hostage, but God protected us, and we were rescued. When I was seven years old, I lived through an earthquake that caused my school to collapse, and almost one hundred schoolgirls died that day. My home was full of domestic violence. I grew up seeing war, pain, loss, poverty, and a lack of fathers. It was scenery void of peace. But when I had an encounter with God, I found Jesus. His love was overwhelming, and He captured my heart. My life was transformed as I experienced the Father's love. I felt the peace of God in my life for the first time.

Throughout our lives, we receive promises from God—promises of healing, restoration, and transformation. We might receive promises like Abraham and Sarah's. They were promised children. During their waiting period they lost their peace. Sarah became desperate, so she tried to help God. It's never wise to run ahead of God. In the process, Abraham had a child, but with Hagar. When Sarah felt weak, frustrated, and anxious and had lost faith, our promise-keeping God visited her. She conceived Isaac, her long-awaited son, who brought her joy and lots of laughter.

When the circumstances of life seem chaotic, I've learned that I can choose peace in His presence where I can be assured that He has everything under control.

Years have gone by since I first invited the Prince of Peace to rule in my heart, and I've faced many unique circumstances. As a missionary in Guatemala, I serve people with addictions and broken hearts. The Holy Spirit goes with us to the darkest places and sends His love as He transforms lives, bringing peace as we minister His grace. We are seeing salvations and healing. Even with the present restrictions, He is giving us creative ways to share His love.

Beyond my childhood trauma and the sometimes heart-wrenching ministry encounters, one of my most challenging struggles has been infertility. This longing for parenthood has been a journey now of almost fifteen years. It has been surrounded by ongoing tests and words about impossibilities—not encouraging reports. In God's presence, I've always found His peace that surpasses all understanding (Philippians 4:6–7). Speaking to Him and seeking His face brings a fresh revelation of His love. Though I am without children right now, I still have His peace. I hold to the truth that He has good plans for me that will continue to give me hope and a future, and I am trusting Him in how He will fulfill His promise.

I want to encourage you—don't allow any circumstance to steal your peace. Keep chasing and pursuing Him and be intentional to walk in His peace. The Bible is clear when it says God can do infinitely more, exceedingly abundantly above all that we ask or think. I praise God for His faithfulness in my life. His hand snatched me from the hostage takers; He protected me through war. The earthquake didn't swallow me up; disappointments have not crushed me; restrictions have not limited His work; the trials I've had to endure have made me stronger. Praise God, He's still writing my story!

Jesus, I'm encouraged today that you are on my side. You have been so faithful to watch over me in every way. Where I am still "trying to make sense" of things, thank you for always welcoming me into your presence with love and understanding. You are still in control.

Unwavering Peace

Day Twenty-Nine
Contributed by Ruth Paul

"The name of the Lord is a fortified tower; the righteous run to it and are safe."
—Proverbs 18:10

Our son, Andrew, was just five when he began repeatedly complaining of stomach aches. A few months passed before it dawned on me that this was a recurring issue. We could never have imagined that a simple check-up with the doctor would begin an eighteen-month journey of specialists, bloodwork, and numerous tests.

Eventually, Andrew was admitted to a nearby children's hospital for more tests and a biopsy. The news was staggering. We weren't dealing with a stomachache; we were dealing with a tumour. Tests revealed that the source of his chronic ill health was a tumour in his ankle. It would take nine long months to determine the best course of action.

My husband, Roger, and I obviously had many sobering and heart-wrenching discussions. We'd heard the statistics of couples who have a sick child and the strain it puts on a marriage. We chose to go through this together with God as our anchor. We talked about songs that we had sung in church for years, songs about God being our strong tower and peace in a storm, about Him never leaving us, about His goodness. We realized this was the time to either walk in what we'd been singing about or walk away. Either it was true, or it wasn't—and we both knew it was.

The most difficult part of the journey was making the decision about how to remove the tumour. It was a very entangled mass that wrapped itself like knotted tentacles around bones and vessels in the foot. Doctors soon realized that none of the usual treatments, or even surgery, would be effective in Andrew's situation to maintain an active lifestyle. The best option was amputation.

We knew little about amputation and what future life would look like for Andrew. We were making a life altering decision for our son, and we didn't know how to decide. In meeting with our pastor, we were reminded that God is sovereign. He can see the future that we cannot, and sometimes as parents we must make difficult decisions. Pastor encouraged us that divine intervention wouldn't be limited by our choice to move forward. God could change the picture at any time. We felt a tangible peace, and we knew we must proceed. It became clear to us both that amid the storm, the simple truth was that "God's got this. He can step in at any time and change it. He is with you; God isn't restricted by time." It settled our souls with the peace needed to move forward.

It's an unusual thing to have a conversation with a six-year-old about his own below-the-knee amputation, but we did it with God's grace and peace. We were able to surround Andrew with an atmosphere of confidence in God's presence, reminding him too of God's love and ability to heal. We carried the peace God gave us through the months leading to the surgery and during the surgery. Within twenty-four hours in recovery, we knew we'd made the right decision. We could see the colour and health returning to Andrew.

Eight months after his surgery, Andrew was playing Pee-Wee football. That was just the beginning of the active, full life he continues to lead—a college graduate who runs basketball boot camps across the region and (when Covid clears) will be taking his skills to assist a mission organization in Uganda!

Oswald Chambers once said, "Whenever His hand is laid upon you, it gives inexpressible peace and comfort, and the sense that 'underneath are the everlasting arms,' (Deuteronomy 33:27) full of support, provision, comfort and strength."[15] Be encouraged today that God's peace that surpasses all understanding is available as your place of safety and assurance as you navigate uncharted waters in your life.

Heavenly Father, it's hard to imagine such an unwavering peace. Sometimes I let trivial things steal my peace. I repent for needlessly making parts of my daily life into dilemmas. Restore my heart to a place of resting in your truth. Amen.

---

15 "85 Quotes about Peace," *Christian Quotes*, accessed November 14, 2020, https://www.christianquotes.info/quotes-by-topic/quotes-about-peace/.

Believing for Transformation

Day Thirty

"Follow the example of all that we have imparted to you and the God of peace will be with you in all things."

—Philippians 4:9, TPT

We have now journeyed together for thirty days in this search to discover a greater understanding of His peace. We have traversed landscapes of life that have pictured for us the work of the Holy Spirit on the life of a believer as we believe and receive God's gift of peace through Jesus. We have been reminded that it is possible to experience peace on the inside in varied and unexpected circumstances, see peace restored, practise His presence, and grow into relationships of peace with others. While we have looked, with encouragement, at biblical personalities and events, many of this "company of friends" have also drawn your attention to powerful truths about peace in specific Bible verses they have highlighted. While doing so, they have drawn back the curtain on the stage of their lives, sharing their unique peace encounters in their personal pilgrimages.

As we come into right relationship with God, a soundness or wholeness influences and directs our thoughts and behaviour. This wholeness not only helps us to walk in security and trust in His faithfulness and His promises, but it stands guard during attacks of loneliness, illness, financial hardship, loss, anxiety, disappointment, and transition.

Allow the truths in these devotionals to saturate your spirit over the next days and weeks. Renew your commitment to walk in His peace. Use these simple prayers from each contribution, and watch a holy transformation take place. I like what Bill Johnson says in his devotional *Hosting the Presence Every Day*: "Every peace-filled moment you experience brings terror to the powers of darkness ... in an atmosphere of peace, darkness cannot prevail ... Where his presence is, there is peace."[16] Let's determine to live in His presence, in the righteousness, peace, and joy of the kingdom, shifting atmospheres, walking in wholeness and victory, transformed by His truth.

I speak shalom to you as you continue to navigate through these challenging but exhilarating days journeying with Him. *"The Lord bless you and keep you; the Lord make his face shine on you and be gracious to you; the Lord turn his face toward you and give you peace,"* (Numbers 6:24–26).

Like a River Glorious
Like a river glorious is God's perfect peace,
Over all victorious, in its bright increase;
Perfect, yet it floweth fuller every day,
Perfect, yet it groweth deeper all the way.
Refrain:
Stayed upon Jehovah, hearts are fully blest
Finding, as He promised, perfect peace and rest.
Hidden in the hollow of His blessed hand,
Never foe can follow, never traitor stand;
Not a surge of worry, not a shade of care,
Not a blast of hurry touch the spirit there.
Refrain:
Stayed upon Jehovah, hearts are fully blest
Finding, as He promised, perfect peace and rest.[17]

---

16 Bill Johnson, "July 7," *Hosting the Presence Every Day: 365 Days to Unveiling Heaven's Agenda for Your Life*, Kindle edition.

17 Frances R. Havergal, "Like a River Glorious," *Hymnal.net*, accessed December 21, 2020, https://www.hymnal.net/en/hymn/h/719.

Small Group Helps

This devotional journey welcomes the participation of others in a small group setting, either in person or online. A four-week group session, meeting once weekly, is recommended. Each participant will need their own copy of the book and can journal any take-aways or questions from their daily readings. In a small group setting, all participants should be reading the devotional entries at the same time so that discussions centre around the same readings on any given week. Discussing your insights will reveal some impacting and exciting truths.

The group leader may select two to five questions from the following list for the weekly group meeting, which should run between sixty and seventy minutes. Vary your selection of questions from the list, adapting them to your group's focus. Be sure to allow time for personal thoughts, testimonies of growth, and any questions. Keep a scriptural view as foundational and expect God to meet with you as you gather. The preferred leadership style for this topic is facilitation, where the leader encourages both participation and time boundaries during sharing. The facilitator should be familiar with the material and keep the discussion moving.

Discussion Questions (Choose your own adventure!)

- Which biblical character or event was most impactful to your growth this week?
- What life lesson did you learn from that character or event?
- Which testimony stood out for you this week? Share what you gained from it.

- Share one truth or lesson that might be relevant to pass along to a specific friend in the near future.
- Choose a scripture verse from this week's devotionals and unpack what it means in your life right now.
- Talk about your most repeated peace stealer and allow the group to pray for you. (One or two each week could do this.)
- Which relational struggle (i.e. unforgiveness, jealousy, resentment, injustice, unfairness, negativity, gossip, belittlement, rejection, control, ingratitude, etc.) do you relate to the most and why?
- Jesus is always ready to help us, but we must be willing to ask. What is your most difficult ask and why?
- Comment on this statement: "If I could really believe His promises, I could trust."
- Is forgiveness a key to peace that I have not utilized well? Who do I need to forgive?
- God wants to give us peace during troubles. Where are you believing for greater peace this week?
- If God spoke to you today about freedom from your fears and limitations, what would He be saying to you? What would the new you look like?
- In what area of your life do you need more shalom? *- weight, family.*
- What are some of the negative thought patterns that need to change in your life? Listen to the Holy Spirit and suggest some new truths and declarations that He is directing you to make.
- Since God doesn't often tell us how He will fulfill His promises, how can we 1) find peace and 2) stay in faith when we have no sense of what's coming next? *- His Word*
- Keep a list of wins this week in the area of finding peace and be ready to share some of those wins next week.
- Where has God used you in the past few weeks to impart peace into a situation?
- Come next week with a scripture that expresses God's unshakeable peace and unpack it for your group members.
- How is righteousness connected to peace and joy in your life?

Who we are in Christ
Our identity in Him

- What are some key rewards for the peacemaker?
- If you're in "wait mode" right now for a particular promise God has given you, is there anything about your present response pattern that needs to change to align with the purposes of God?
- Where do you need to allow peace to be an umpire?
- How important is "process" in the overall plan of God? Explain.   Trust
- If you have experienced a significant loss, share with the group some ways they could be helpful in protecting your peace.
- If you are experiencing a seeming "dead end" to a dream or a plan, but are still standing on the truth of God's promises, like Christal or Karla, share with the group how they can help you.
- If you have been looking to the wrong source for your peace, share what God is showing you.
- What do you need to do to see greater peace in financial areas?

Trust in His promises.

Week Five

If the group would like to add a summary week (a fifth week), we suggest each participant come with a brief testimony related to their growth and revelation in this journey toward peace and that the group give time to celebration and prayer for one another. Be sure to invite all group members to experience personal salvation and have a time of prayer for family situations in which there is chaos or uncertainty.

Note: As a bonus, for the first eighteen months after release, contact the author at ruth.teakle@gmail.com to have one of the contributors as a guest (online only) at one of your group sessions. Details upon request.

Lisa's Cell:
Frank.

-705 -386 -1999.
Tues,
9-3

Contributors

Judy Chiarot co-pastored Faith Family Church with her husband, Paul, in Beamsville for twenty-five years, where their ministry took them to several nations to bless and encourage local churches. In her present capacity on the Board of Directors for Anchor Ministerial Fellowship, she and Paul provide inspiration and assistance to Anchor pastors across Ontario. At her local church, she serves in prayer and prophetic encouragement. Judy desires to see believers prepared for ministry and actively building up Christ's body (Ephesians 4:12). Judy and Paul have three children and three grandchildren and reside in Hamilton, Ontario.

Abby Clattenburg is a lover of Jesus and the local church. She was born into a pastor's home and has loved and served Jesus all her life. Recently married and residing in Beamsville, Ontario, she and her husband, Levi, love to worship together and serve people with a heart of compassion. Abby is an entrepreneur and a gifted worship leader, songwriter, and musician. Helping people discover their destiny throu' ing, prayer, and a listening ear, Abby is a trusted and valuable c team environments. www.lakemount.ca

Stephanie Courtney lives in Sarnia, Ontario with her husband, Caleb, and four children: Olivia, Samuel, Marcus, and Joel. Caleb and Stephanie have each been leading worship and music ministries in Ontario PAOC churches for over twenty years. Following a fifteen-year tenure as an elementary teacher, Stephanie is now a full-time stay-at-home mom. She's passionate about her volunteer work at the local pregnancy centre and oversees the worship ministry at her home church, Bethel Pentecostal Church, in Sarnia.

Whether Sue Keddy is sitting in the squalor of a Vietnamese refugee camp, a dilapidated shack in Haiti, a courtyard in the northwest frontier of Pakistan, the needle-strewn floor of a hovel in the inner city, or a palatial mansion overlooking the South China Sea, and whether she's standing in front of one person in the grocery store line or before thousands, her heart pounds to make her Jesus famous. Her heart's cry is for everyone to know His love, peace, and nearness. Her prayer is to be the hands, feet, and the heart of Jesus to the lost, lonely, broken, and forgotten, wherever Jesus takes her.

www.dreambigwithus.org

Betty Ann Lewis was born in Newfoundland, the daughter of Salvation Army officers. She and her husband, Doug, retired following forty years of ministry as Salvation Army officers throughout Canada, Germany, the Bahamas, and Bermuda. Betty Ann enjoys volunteer involvement in the local Rotary and Probus and serves as part of the spiritual care on-call at the Royal Victoria Hospital. She oversees the community care at the Salvation Army in Barrie and conducts services at various seniors' residences. Betty Ann and Doug take great joy in family, treasuring four sons, seven grandchildren, and one great-grandchild.

Ruth Paul is a mother of two young adult children, Andrew and Angela. Originally from the United States, she has made Canada her home since moving from the States to marry her late husband, Roger, in 1991. Having obtained an Associate in Theology degree from Ambassador College, Ruth has worked at Lakemount Worship Centre since 2002 in a variety of administrative and pastoral roles. Her joy in ministry is watching people's lives change as they grow in the knowledge of who God is and who they are because of His love for them. Ruth enjoys reading and baking chocolate chip cookies!

Cheryl-Ann Philip is a chemistry graduate of the University of Toronto. She has travelled extensively to aid in humanitarian relief and volunteered with Big Sisters of Peel and the Philip Aziz Centre for Hospice Care. After a decade in telecommunications sales support, she transitioned to the charitable space, planning and overseeing international events. She's an entrepreneur, visionary, and advocate for personal wellness. Cheryl-Ann is a founding member and managing director for Truth Nation, a charity group specializing in community wellness events.

www.truthnation.ca

Vinetta Sanderson, an ordained minister with the PAOC, resides in Armstrong, British Columbia alongside family. Her life has been a beautiful tapestry of ministry alongside her late husband, Ira, sharing her musical talents, preaching, and ministering in pastoral care. Past roles have included Executive Assistant and Office Administrator for Women Alive and pastoring at Kitchener Gospel Temple. Vinetta is well known as a speaker who carries a message of hope and healing, born out of God's faithfulness during significant personal loss. She enjoys grandparenting, writing, and music, and she insists that celebrating Christmas requires much more than twelve days.

Karla Stoffelsen, BTh, is co-founder of House of Refuge Street Ministries in Guatemala. She grew up in El Salvador and responded to the call of God in 2006 when she married her husband, Steven Stoffelsen. Karla reaches out to women trapped in human trafficking, prostitution, and poverty. She is a fire-filled preacher/missionary/pastor who shares the gospel together with her husband in Guatemala, El Salvador, Honduras, Mexico, Canada, and the USA. She believes that signs and wonders follow the believer.

www.houseofrefuge.ca

Janet Soppitt moved to Canada from the UK in 2005 with her husband and five children. She has been both a home-schooling mum and pastor's wife. She holds degrees from Oxford Brooks University, England in both English and Geography, and a Post-Graduate Certificate of Education from Oxford. Janet is currently teaching English and physical education at Niagara Christian Collegiate, where she passionately shares God's love with others, encouraging them to live out the abundant life promised in Jesus. Janet has served the community as a regional athletics coach and is a gifted motivational speaker and professional life coach.

Marion Venables is a retired Salvation Army officer. She married her husband, Gary, also an officer, fifty-three years ago, whom she met in the Salvation Army College for Officers. Their forty-four years of service provided varied opportunities to serve across Canada as pastors/officers in corps/church, youth work, college staff, the Six Nations, and in Canadian territorial and divisional appointments. Marion and Gary continue to serve within the Salvation Army church community of London Citadel. They have three children and eight grandchildren.

Christal Wilson MDiv., R.P was born in Ottawa, Ontario. She's a Registered Psychotherapist and marriage counsellor. In 2020, she started a private practice, and she serves beautiful people from all over Canada through the wonder of technology. Christal loves to travel and also feels at home in her church, Lakemount Worship Centre, where she serves in prayer ministry and worship leading. She speaks and teaches about her passions for mental health, relationships, and life with God.

Following a thirty-four-year elementary school teaching career in Niagara, Virginia Zyta joined a friend in developing an early childhood literacy program for parents and teachers in Peel region. Her career delightfully included a two-year teaching exchange in the United Kingdom and a post-retirement position with ESL international students at Columbia International College. She enjoys extensive travel as well as painting, walking, biking, swimming, gardening, and kayaking. She serves in ministries of prayer and healing at her local church.

About the Author

Ruth Teakle lives with her husband, Carl, in Beamsville, Ontario. She loves to spend time with her three children and their spouses and her eleven grandchildren. Although retired, Ruth serves as a support staff member at Lakemount Worship Centre in Grimsby, Ontario, where she previously served on full-time staff for eighteen years. Her roles varied from overseeing small groups and missions to prayer and pastoral care. As well, she has led and assisted with numerous short-term missions to the Caribbean, Eastern Europe, Ukraine, South America, northern Ontario, and Quebec.

On the home front, Ruth and Carl have fostered over 130 children during a twenty-five-year period. Ruth has worked within the Correctional Services of Canada, led summer camps, and filmed a national training course for telephone prayer partners.

Ruth's academic pursuits have included studies at Lakeshore Teachers' College, Brock University (Bachelor of Arts), and Wagner University (Master of Practical Ministries). She has completed ESL studies and is a Certified Anger Management Specialist. Prior to taking additional Religious Studies courses in preparation for ordained ministry, Ruth enjoyed a successful thirty-two-year career as an elementary school teacher.

Ruth's heart is to see people become passionate followers of Christ—saved, healed, and free. She has a strong sense of mission to help people build healthy connections with God and with others and walk in the fullness of their destiny. Her challenging but victorious personal journey makes her well qualified to share on God's real and unshakeable peace in her third devotional, *Pursuing Peace.*

Additional Note: Ruth's first devotional, *Changing Seasons*, is a pocket/ purse sized devotional full of encouragement from God's Word written especially for seniors and is one of the GODQUEST SERIES available only through The Bible League, Canada.

bibleleague.ca/resources/godquest/

Pursuing Patience and *Pursuing Peace* are available through Word Alive Press and numerous national and international outlets. As well, watch for the next devotional in the series, *Choosing Love*, coming this spring, 2021.